KOREAN *KAYAGŬM SANJO*:
A TRADITIONAL INSTRUMENTAL GENRE

Korean *Kayagŭm Sanjo*:
A Traditional Instrumental Genre

KEITH HOWARD
School of Oriental and African Studies, University of London, UK

CHAESUK LEE
Seoul National University and Hanyang University, South Korea

NICHOLAS CASSWELL
University of Central Lancashire, UK

ASHGATE

Published by
Ashgate Publishing Limited
Gower House
Croft Road
Aldershot
Hampshire GU11 3HR
England

Ashgate Publishing Company
Suite 420
101 Cherry Street
Burlington, VT 05401-4405
USA

Ashgate website: http://www.ashgate.com

British Library Cataloguing in Publication Data
Howard, Keith, 1956–
    Korean *kayagŭm sanjo* : a traditional instrumental genre
    1. Lee, Chaesuk 2. Sanjo (Folk music) – History and
    criticism 3. Kayagŭm music 4. Music – Philosophy and
    aesthetics 5. Kayagŭm – History 6. Kayagŭm players – Korea
    (South) – Biography
    I. Title II. Lee, Chaesuk III. Casswell, Nicholas
    787.7'09519

Library of Congress Cataloging-in-Publication Data
Howard, Keith, 1956–
    Korean *kayagŭm sanjo* : a traditional instrumental genre / by Keith Howard,
Chaesuk Lee, and Nicholas Casswell.
        p. cm. – (SOAS musicology series)
    Includes bibliographical references (p. 145), discography (p. 153), and index.
    ISBN 978-0-7546-6362-1 (alk. paper)
1. Sanjo (Folk music) – Korea (South) – History and criticism.
2. Kayagŭm – Korea (South) I. Lee, Chaesuk, 1941–
II. Casswell, Nicholas, 1974– III. Title.

ML3752.H694 2007
784.162'957–dc22

2007029823

ISBN 978-0-7546-6362-1

Printed and bound in Great Britain by MPG Books Ltd, Bodmin, Cornwall.

Contents

List of Figures and Table

Figures

Table

List of Notations

CD Contents

CD 1 (SOASIS 07): *Kayagŭm Sanjo*

Kim Chukp'a School, performed by Chaesuk Lee, *Kayagŭm*, and Kim Sunok, *Changgo*

1	*Tasŭrŭm*	2.29
2	*Chinyangjo*	22.55
3	*Chungmori*	10.12
4	*Chungjungmori*	2.58
5	*Chajinmori*	4.06
6	*Hwimori*	8.17
7	*Sesanjoshi*	4.00

CD 2 (SOASIS 09): *Kŏmun'go Sanjo*

Shin K'waedong's School, performed by Kim Sunok, *Kŏmun'go* and *Changgo*

1	*Chinyangjo*	15.22
2	*Chungmori*	16.45
3	*Ŏnmori*	2.16
4	*Chungjungmori*	3.17
5	*Chajinmori*	8.23

Notes on the Performers

Chaesuk Lee entered Seoul National University to study Korean music in 1959, the year that the first degree course began, taking the *kayagŭm* zither as her major. She was the first to gain an MA in Korean music, and gave a landmark recital on the zither in 1964 that included pieces from all three repertories – court music, folk music and new compositions. She was the first woman to be appointed a professor of Korean music, and in 1994 established the Korean Zither Musicians Association. She has been the recipient of numerous awards during her career, and in 2004 was elected a member of the National Academy of Arts. (See Chapter 3 for a comprehensive biography.)

Kim Sunok is a performance lecturer at Ewha Women's University and the Korean National University of the Arts. She graduated with BA and MA degrees from Seoul National University in 1987 and 1997 respectively, and has recently completed her PhD at Ewha Women's University. She is well known as a *kŏmun'go* six-stringed zither and *changgo* hourglass-shaped drum performer, and since her solo debut in 1988 has given performances in Korea, China, Japan, Vietnam, and in America in Hawai'i, San Francisco, Chicago, Michigan, Detroit and Washington.

Acknowledgements

Chapter 2 is based on two earlier papers, Keith Howard's 'The Korean *kayagŭm*: the making of a zither', formerly published in *Papers of the British Association for Korean Studies* 5 (1994): 1–22, and Chaesuk Lee's 'The development of the construction and performance techniques of the *kayagŭm*', formerly published in Nathan Hesselink, ed., *Contemporary Directions: Korean Folk Music Engaging the Twentieth Century and Beyond*: 96–120 (Berkeley: Center for Korean Studies, University of California, Berkeley, 2001). The notation of Kim Chukp'a's *kayagŭm sanjo* was formerly published by Chaesuk Lee, as *Kayagŭm sanjo, Kim Chukp'a ryu/Kayagum Sanjo of Kim, Chuk-Pa School with Changgo accompaniment* (Seoul: Susŏwŏn, 1983); it has been updated and prepared for publication here by Nicholas Casswell. We thank Kim Sunok and Chaesuk Lee for giving permission to include their recordings of *kayagŭm sanjo* and *kŏmun'go sanjo* with this book. The CDs were recorded and mastered by Jeremy Glasgow, and CD production was overseen by Andrea Hector-Watkins. Sections of Chapters 4 and 5 were presented at the 2005 British Forum for Ethnomusicology conference in London and at an AHRC Research Centre symposium held at SOAS. We thank the many colleagues who have made constructive comments on our research.

Preface

The Korean genre of *sanjo* is today one of the most popular genres of traditional music, taught in schools and universities within Korea, and a staple of national and international performance tours. *Sanjo* comprises a set of related pieces for solo melodic instrument and drum. A number of 'schools' (*ryu*) are recognized, each based on the performance style of a master musician, usually a musician from an earlier generation. *Sanjo* was first devised for the *kayagŭm*, a 12-stringed plucked long zither with roots stretching back almost two thousand years that today is arguably the most popular of Korea's melodic instruments.

Sanjo is now played on all major Korean instruments: *kŏmun'go* six-stringed plucked long zither, *ajaeng* seven- or eight-stringed bowed long zither, *haegŭm* two-stringed fiddle, *p'iri* oboe, *taegŭm* transverse bamboo flute, *soaenap* shawm (also known as the *saenap*, *nallari* and *hŏjŏk*), and *tanso* and *t'ungso* vertical notched flutes. In *sanjo*, the solo melodic instrument is accompanied by a drum; normally the accompanist plays the *changgo* double-headed hourglass-shaped drum that is ubiquitous to so many genres of Korean music. The two Sino-Korean characters that comprise the term '*sanjo*' can be translated as 'scattered melodies', but such a translation hardly does justice to the complexity of *sanjo*: each piece, played in entirety, can last for an hour, although in concerts players will often choose segments from this long piece to fit a specified time frame.

Exploring *Kayagŭm Sanjo*

Amongst contemporary performers, Chaesuk Lee has done much to develop our understanding of *sanjo*. In her career, she has combined scholarly research with performing. One of the first students of the Seoul National University programme in *kugak*, Korean traditional music, and the first female professor of *kugak* in Korea, she worked with the most senior master musicians of *kayagŭm sanjo*, chief amongst them Kim Chukp'a (1911–89). Kim was the granddaughter of the putative founder of *sanjo*, Kim Ch'angjo. Kim Chukp'a had been a celebrated performer in her youth, but she retired as a professional musician in the early 1930s when she married her first husband. Lee began to study with her in 1967, and was instrumental in encouraging her to return to public life when her second husband died in the 1970s. Lee has perhaps been most influential through her development of notations for the major schools of *kayagŭm sanjo* that remain in use today.

This volume explores, records, notates and documents the Kim Chukp'a school of *kayagŭm sanjo*. It is the result of a collaboration between Chaesuk Lee, the ethnomusicologist Keith Howard and the composer and musicologist Nicholas Casswell. Although both Howard and Casswell worked with Lee in Korea during earlier studies of Korean music, research for this book and the recording of the two accompanying CDs began in 2004, when Lee and her colleague Kim Sunok were invited as resident research fellows to the School of Oriental and African Studies (SOAS) within the University of London. Kim Sunok is central to the accompanying CDs, as both drum accompanist and *kŏmun'go* player. In London, Lee and Kim gave two concerts, one at the South Bank with the Korean Zither Musicians Association – a group established by Lee in 1994 – and one at SOAS in which they both gave full *sanjo* performances. Lee's performance of the Kim Chukp'a *kayagŭm sanjo* was subsequently recorded, with Kim Sunok accompanying, in the AHRC recording studio at SOAS; the second CD contained here illustrates an additional *sanjo* school played by Kim Sunok on a second instrument, the *kŏmun'go* six-stringed zither.

Chapter 1 provides a history of *sanjo*, so far as it is known, discussing potential precursors and related genres, detailing the musicians known for *sanjo* mastery, and exploring how, from its first incarnation as a piece for the *kayagŭm*, schools and versions for other instruments evolved. Chapter 2 gives an overview of the *kayagŭm* itself, in its past and present forms. A biography of Chaesuk Lee is offered in Chapter 3, and then, forming the core of the volume, we present two extended analyses. Chapter 4 essentially explores rhythm and mode, reflecting on potential and real connections between *sanjo* and *p'ansori* (epic storytelling through song), and links to region and dialect. We present a descriptive analysis, founded on Korean musicological scholarship but infused with the perceptions of musicians whom Chaesuk Lee has worked with – particularly Kim Chukp'a – that seeks to combine ethnomusicological methodology and Korean musicology. We recognize, however, the contrasting approaches – Korean musicology is framed by a methodology that has developed since the late 1950s and which has been highly successful at elevating traditional Korean music to an icon of identity, while ethnomusicology has been particularly influenced by thinking in anthropology – hence Chapter 5 presents a very different analysis. We ask whether Deleuzian and Guattarian thinking on music, framed by plateaus ten and eleven of their *A Thousand Plateaus*, and a philosophy never to our knowledge previously applied to Korean music, can offer a new way of understanding the structure of *sanjo* that avoids reification and abstraction into musical elements such as mode, rhythm or melody. This, in a manner that the late Mantle Hood might have accepted into his 'QTM' (the so-called 'quantum theory of music'), will, we hope, encourage others to take studies of *sanjo* forward.

The AHRC Research Centre Series

This volume is published as part of a series sponsored by the AHRC Research Centre for Cross-Cultural Music and Dance Performance. The Research Centre was established in September 2002 as a joint venture between SOAS, the University of Surrey and Roehampton University, funded by the (British) Arts and Humanities Research Council. The Centre explores questions raised by the performance of music and movement, and their interrelationships, in artistic practice beyond the European art- and popular-music canons. To do so, it seeks to establish: a synthesis between the performance concerns of western musicological research and ethnomusicology, exploring and addressing a discrete set of activities that have performance at their core; methodologies and techniques utilized in the analysis of Western theatre and dance performance and in dance anthropological research to evaluate their appropriateness and efficacy in resolving research questions that have performance at their core; acknowledgement of common music and dance concerns of cultural coding – aspects of movement or sound performance determined by social and cultural contexts. This approach shifts the focus of study to take on board and explain the perceptions of performers from Asia and Africa about their own music and dance, and about its transformations and adaptations, combining these with systems of analysis and description. This is precisely what we do in this volume by combining the expertise and experience of Chaesuk Lee with a survey of relevant Korean musicological scholarship, and by juxtaposing two contrasting analytical chapters in an attempt to move our understanding forward from existing Korean and foreign research on *sanjo*.

Each volume in the series celebrates one or more musicians and dancers, presenting detailed discussions of training, context and repertory. Each is the result of a collaborative research project, in which performers have worked alongside academics to record, edit and master audio or audio-visual materials, and have discussed at length their backgrounds, experience and their understanding of the music or dance for which they are famous. Our intention is not to offer an overview of a single music culture, nor to present an exhaustive account of, say, 'Korean music'; many other publications do this, most recently the *Global Music Series* from Oxford University Press edited by Bonnie Wade and Patricia Shehan Campbell (published from 2004 onwards). Rather, we want to bring these master musicians and dancers to readers, listeners and viewers, allowing them a voice while at the same time unravelling salient aspects of their performances.

Why? Well, the world is getting smaller. While ethnomusicologists and dance anthropologists have, rightly, prided themselves on conducting fieldwork among responsive musicians and dancers in obscure and remote places, the artists all too often remain distant to the resulting ethnographic representations. With Airbus and Boeing competing to produce ever-larger airplanes, this approach is no longer tenable. Musicians and dancers, just as do scholars, travel the world. 'There is no they there' famously wrote Jody Diamond (1990); Paul Simon on *Graceland* sings: 'These are the days of lasers in the jungle / This is the long-distance call'. Steven Feld reminds us of the 'complex traffic in sounds, money and media' (Keil and Feld 1994: 238; see also Feld 1996).

Many ethnomusicologists and dance anthropologists would claim that their ethnographies offer faithful accounts, painstakingly collected, checked and cross-referenced against all available materials, publications and archives. In some cases, cross-referencing requires a return to the field, to allow reflection and, perhaps, additional discussion and deliberation. In the 1980s and 1990s, many trumpeted the benefits of 'emic' accounts, by, for example, Hugo Zemp (1981), Steven Feld (1982) and Marina Roseman (1991). They talked about how to capture what musicians and dancers thought about their performance arts and how to translate the metaphors they used into a familiar language. Accounts tended to follow trends in anthropology, often with a touch of delay, and so music and dance was discussed as if confined by its locale, with populations largely considered impervious to the global media or resisting change, maintaining and conserving their traditions. This was ably suggested in 1981, when the International Folk Music Council renamed itself, in Seoul, at the very meeting where Howard and Lee first met, as the International Council for Traditional Music.

By the 1990s, calls to preserve music and dance were becoming louder. Following Alan Lomax (1985: 40–46), cultural diversity was celebrated, and the standardization of culture by the global media and produced for us rather than by us was questioned. What better way of celebrating diversity than allowing musicians and dancers a voice? How, though, can scholars trained in the West meet those from the East and share ownership of a resulting account? If collaborative efforts are to be meaningful, this series has to be sufficiently flexible not to impose a single approach. And so, while some volumes will present detailed analysis, others will offer a comprehensive account of a specific repertory as maintained or developed by one or more musicians or dancers. Again, some volumes will focus on 'tradition' (and one or more of the potential meanings that such a troublesome term has) or on repertories that have not been adequately documented, but others will explore globalization and the way that musicians and dancers from one place interact and work with those from another.

This, volume, then, celebrates a specific Korean music genre, *sanjo*, as developed and played on a specific instrument, the *kayagŭm*, focussing on a master musician who developed a specific school of *kayagŭm sanjo*, Kim Chukp'a, as studied, internalized, and performed by Chaesuk Lee.

Notes on Romanization

As with most publications by foreign scholars on Korea, we use the McCune-Reischauer romanization system for Korean terms, but as modified by the Korean Ministry of Education in 1988 ('shi' rather than 'si', to reflect pronunciation). An exception to this is personal names. Names given in Korean in published sources are rendered here in McCune-Reischauer, without hyphenation, but we respect preferred spellings of personal names where the publication is in English or another European language. In the text and index we also respect preferred spellings where the person is known beyond Korea, where a publication or album is distributed in the international market, or where a person has communicated a clear preference. We give McCune-Reischauer equivalents in square brackets on the first occurrence of a person's name only where this facilitates crosschecking. Pyongyang and Seoul are the accepted romanizations for the capitals of the Democratic People's Republic of Korea (North Korea) and the Republic of Korea (South Korea). The list of references gives English translations for books and journal articles only where these are provided in the publication. The primary purpose of adopting these slightly cumbersome conventions is to allow readers access in the most reliable way to the cited books, journals and recordings in Korean and non-Korean libraries. We, like most scholars, are reluctant to use the 'new' romanization system currently promoted from Seoul. We do not dispute that this system works for Koreans, but it relies on syllabary that too often has unfortunate connotations for those brought up speaking European languages, thereby undermining efforts to promote Korea to an international audience. We also consider it prudent to retain the McCune-Reischauer system since, as we go to press, Korean discussion groups are once more debating moves to yet again change the romanization system.

Chapter 1

The Genre: *Kayagŭm Sanjo*

The Korean genre of *sanjo* comprises a set of related pieces for solo melodic instrument and drum. Here we are concerned with *sanjo* for the 12-stringed plucked long zither, *kayagŭm*, the instrument for which it was first devised. While the two Sino-Korean characters that comprise the term can be translated as 'scattered melodies', some scholars consider that this designation evolved from a purely Korean term, *hŏt'ŭn karak*, 'loosely organized melodies' (for example, Song 1986: 95). This begins to offer an explanation for structure, though, as we note in the Preface to this volume, it hardly does justice to the complexity of a piece that, played in entirety, can last for an hour. A performance of a full *kayagŭm sanjo* – such as that recorded by Chaesuk Lee on the first CD (SOASIS-07) included with this volume – begins with what was once a tuning and adjustment section, the nonmetrical *tasŭrŭm*. For all *sanjo* versions on all instruments, the initial substantial movement that follows the *tasŭrŭm* employs a slow but steadily repeating 18/8 rhythmic cycle, *chinyangjo* – note that, as with Kim Sunok's performance of *kŏmun'go sanjo* recorded on the second CD (SOASIS-08) included with this volume, *sanjo* played on instruments other than the *kayagŭm* often do not incorporate the *tasŭrŭm* section. The *chinyangjo* movement is the emotional core of the genre and may take half of the total performance time. The music segues through a series of increasingly faster movements in compound metres, each following, and each named after, a specific rhythmic cycle: the medium-paced *chungmori* (12/4), moderately fast *chungjungmori* (12/8) and the fast *chajinmori* (12/8). Sometimes, *chungjungmori* is missing, and additional movements may be included based on rhythmic cycles such as *kutkŏri* (6/8+6/8), *hwimori* (12/8), *ŏnmori* (5/8+5/8) and so on. Typically, the music resolves with a very fast movement that replaces compound metre with duple time – *hwimori* (4/4), *tanmori* (4/4) or *sesanjoshi* (4/4).[1]

Different *sanjo* pieces are associated with great players from earlier generations, and are defined in terms of 'schools' (*ryu*; using a term adopted from Japan) named after them. Today, *sanjo* features prominently in the Republic of Korea's preservation system, as Intangible Cultural Properties (*Muhyŏng munhwajae*) 16, 23 and 45, for *kŏmun'go*, *kayagŭm* and *taegŭm* respectively.[2] In the 1960s and 1970s, as the system was established, preservation required research to establish lineage and history. Research by scholars and others was published primarily in a series of reports used to justify nominations – the Cumulative Research Reports on Intangible Cultural Properties (*Chungyo muhyŏng munhwajae*

---

[1]   Note that *hwimori* can denote a 12/8 or a 4/4 rhythmic cycle.

[2]   See Chapter 3 in Howard's *Preserving Korean Music* (2006).

chosa pogosŏ). This research provides a solid basis for our knowledge of the development of *sanjo* and its key performers, although a considerable amount of more detailed work has appeared in subsequent years. At the same time, *sanjo*, formerly taught by rote, in the 1960s became a standard part of instrumental training at colleges and universities. This led to the development of scorebooks and notations tied to analyses (for example Chaesuk Lee 1971, 1979, 1981, 1987; Han Pŏmsu 1975; Kim Taesŏk 1984; Pak Pŏmhun 1985; Kim Haesuk 1987; Ch'oe T'aehyŏn 1988; Mun Chaesuk 1989; Kim Injae 1990). In the late 1970s, an ensemble version of *sanjo* also evolved, linked to but at times replacing the concert form of the improvisatory shamanic ensemble, *shinawi;*[3] this was initially closely associated with musicians at the Traditional Music Arts School (Kugak Yesul Hakkyo) and the associated Folk Music Society's Improvisation Ensemble (Minsok Akhoe Shinawi). More recently, composers have written pieces based on *sanjo.*[4] Beginning in 1986 as a commission for the Asian Games in Beijing and developing in the context of music for the 1988 Seoul Olympic Games, the pop musician Kim Soochul (b.1958) has experimented with updating *sanjo* for guitar,[5] while the drummer and SamulNori founder Kim Duk Soo has devised a one-hour-long *sanjo* for the *changgo* drum.

Historical Sketch

Sanjo putatively evolved from genres of music characteristic of Korea's south-western Chŏlla provinces (Pak Hŏnbong 1967: 16; Yi Pohyŏng 1972; Song Bang-song 1986: 92–106; 2000: 277–93). Chŏlla, until 1948 a single province but since then divided into North Chŏlla and South Chŏlla, is in many ways the artistic centre of Korea. It is home not just to musical creativity but to considerable artistic production. Music from Chŏlla is highly emotional, piquant and sorrowful, and it is tempting to find reasons for this in the area's history. Regional factionalism had been established by the fifteenth century, when the scholar T'oegye characterized the people of Chŏlla as 'willows blowing in the wind', but extended further back,

---

[3]   *Shinawi* was appointed Intangible Cultural Property 52 in 1973 on the basis of a report in the Cumulative Research Report series by Pak Hŏnbong. The designated holder (*poyuja*) was the fiddle player Chi Yŏnghŭi (who will also be mentioned at the end of this chapter). When Chi emigrated to Hawai'i in 1975, the appointment was cancelled, reflecting as much ongoing debates about legitimacy that had established little background for *shinawi* as a concert form predating the Japanese colonial period as it did Chi's emigration. Pak was director of the Traditional Music Arts School.

[4]   For example, Lee Geonyong's (b.1947) 'Cello *Sanjo*' (1981), and Yoo Byung-Eun's (b.1952) 'Piano *Sanjo* I' (1988), 'Piano *Sanjo* II' (1994) and '*Sanjo* for Cello and Piano' (1993) (see Yoo 2000: 171–82). See also the compositions by Kim Kukchin for piano, cello and violin recorded on Synnara Music (NSSRCD-027, 2000, and NSSRCD-028, 2000). Composers have written for Korean instruments, and amongst the pieces Yi Haeshik's (b.1943) series modelled on *sanjo* is notable: '*Hŭktam*/Mud Wall' (1969), '*Sang*/Feature' (1977), '*Sultae kut*/Ritual for a Plectrum' (1984) and '*Hodŭgi*/Bark Pipe' (1984).

[5]   Kim's album *Guitar Sanjo* (Living Sound, 2002) includes four of his versions.

for the province had since antiquity seen many turbulent times. It controlled the sea route from China to Japan, and from the kingdom of Paekche that encompassed Chŏlla but stretched northwards, Buddhism and the tea ceremony were exported to Japan in the fifth to seventh centuries. When the Korean king signed a humiliating peace treaty with the Mongols in the thirteenth century, a rebellion by the so-called 'Three Elite Patrols' (Sambyŏlch'o) led to the establishment of a rival state centred on the south-western island of Chindo that briefly controlled much of the Chŏlla coastline. After a siege lasting almost two years, the rebels were ruthlessly put down; two stone-walled fortresses and the grave of Wang On, a relative of King Wŏnjong declared king by the rebels but murdered by loyalists, remain as memorials. Distant parts of Chŏlla thereafter became places of banishment for aristocrats and others who fell out of favour. In 1597–1598, the strait between Chŏlla and Chindo was where the final naval battle in the Japanese Hideyoshi invasion was fought. In 1894, it was from Chŏlla that peasants marched on Seoul in the Tonghak rebellion; after the king called for Chinese support, this led to the Sino-Japanese war. In 1947, it was to the mountains of Chŏlla that left-wing opponents of President Syngman Rhee retreated, and it was there that they were brutally brought to heel.[6] It was from Chŏlla that the first fully democratic leader of Korea, Kim Dae Jung, was elected as president in 1997. Chŏlla remains Korea's main rice cultivation area, but until the 1980s it was distant from the nation's political and economic axis – which runs from the capital Seoul in the north-west to Pusan in the south-east.

Sanjo masters and Korean musicologists typically state that the musical genre of *sanjo* was invented by Kim Ch'angjo (1865–1919),[7] who was born into an aristocratic family in Yŏngam County in today's South Chŏlla province. Rather than 'invention', it is likely that he merely initiated the performance of a solo instrumental piece for the 12-stringed long zither. The association with Kim first appears in print in Ham Hwajin's 1948 text, *Chosŏn ŭmak t'ongnon*. Ham (1884–1949), a musician and scholar, wrote that *sanjo* was devised by Kim from a repertory known as '*shimbanggok*'. An alternative view was put forward by Pak Hŏnbong (1907–1977), an impresario with the pen name Kusan who in 1947 took over from Ham as director of the forerunner to the Traditional Music Arts School, the Headquarters for the Establishment of Traditional Music (Kugak Kŏnsŏl Ponbu). Pak tracks the origin of *sanjo* back to the sixth-century U Rŭk, who was a native of the Kaya tribal confederacy in the south-east of today's Chŏlla.[8] In a celebrated legend, U Rŭk invented the *kayagŭm*.[9] He wrote 12 pieces for the instrument – their titles survive, but no more. The folk music specialist Yi

---

[6]   Some escaped to the southern island of Cheju.

[7]   Other dates are given in some texts, including 1856 for his birth and 1920 for his death.

[8]   Kaya was an ancient confederacy of tribal states in the south-centre of the Korean peninsula (the eastern part of today's South Chŏlla and the west of today's South Kyŏngsang). The confederacy was absorbed by Shilla; the demise of Kŭmgwan Kaya occurred in 532 CE and that of Tae Kaya in 562 CE.

[9]   Pak was not alone in suggesting this long history: a June 1961 concert in Pyongyang featuring *sanjo* was titled 'Celebrating 1,410 years of the music of U Rŭk' (cited in Yang Sŭnghŭi 2001: 104). Note that in Chapter 2 we refer to earlier roots for the zither.

Pohyŏng (b.1937) fuses the two perspectives together in his report on *kayagŭm sanjo*, volume 34 of the Cumulative series:

> There was *sanjo*-like music ... before Kim Ch'angjo. Kim must be placed within the continuous development of *sanjo*. Just as the excellence of Bach's fugues lies in factors such as his great skill at counterpoint, mastery of formal structures, advanced harmonic treatments, and so on, so Kim's great achievement was to establish the overall form of the genre played to this day. (Yi 1972: 18; see also Yi 1980)

There were certainly many proficient nineteenth-century *kayagŭm* players. Lee Hyeku (b.1908), the founder of contemporary Korean musicology, and the performer, composer and scholar Byungki Hwang (b.1936) both cite Ch'oe Ch'ihak, who was active in Masan in the 1840s and was associated with the separate genre of *shimbanggok*. Hwang also names two of Kim's contemporaries, his elder Han Sukku (1849–1934) and Han Tŏngman (1867–1934) who, as revered zither musicians, might also have shaped the genre (Hwang 2001: 36). Yi Pohyŏng charts additional musicians he considers could have played solo zither pieces before Kim: Yu Sŏngch'ŏn from South Chŏlla, Pak Hanyong, Yi Yŏngch'ae and Pak Haksun from North Chŏlla, and Pak P'algwae, Yi Ch'asu and Shim Chŏngsun from the neighbouring province to the north and north-east of Chŏlla, Ch'ungch'ŏng. We know little about these former musicians,[10] but Yi in a later article notes that each taught a form of *sanjo* to later musicians, Yu to his son Yu Taebong, Pak Hanyong to the female Kim Sohŭi (1911–1994; primarily known as a singer of *p'ansori*, a genre of epic storytelling through song), Pak P'algwae and Yi Ch'asu to Pak Sanggŭn (1905–1949), Shim to Shim Sanggŏn (1889–1965) and so on (Yi 2001: 41–53).

At this point, a consideration of *shimbanggok* is in order, to indicate a potential greater history. First, Sŏng Hyŏn's (1439–1504) text, *Yongjae ch'onghwa*, relates Buddhist chanting to shaman rituals and describes *Yŏngsanhoe* – presumably a precursor of the contemporary chamber suite *Yŏngsan hoesang* – as music to accompany dance and song in '*shimbanggok*' style. Later, Yi Ik's (1682–1764) *Sŏngho sasŏl kukcho akchangjo* equates '*shimbanggok*' to shaman music. *Shimbanggok* is normally assumed to be synonymous with *shinbanggok*; note that the common Kyŏngsang term for a shaman is '*shinbang*' and the regular Cheju term '*shimbang*', while '*kok/-gok*' can be rendered as a piece or a composition. '*Shin*' is a Sino-Korean character for 'spirit', and the three syllables of the common term for a shamanic improvisatory ensemble, *shi-na-wi*, can be considered a variation on *shin-an-wi* (Yu and Hong 1968: 5).[11] This leads us in two distinct directions: to shamanism, where ritualists were until the end of the nineteenth century part of a virtually outcast status group, the *ch'ŏnmin*; and to local literati ensembles that played a precursor of *Yŏngsan hoesang* typically known as *Chul p'ungnyu* or *Hyangje chul p'ungnyu*. This latter, far from being associated with

---

[10]   In respect of which, by way of confirmation, see Kim Haesuk 1987: 122.

[11]   Yi Hyegu (1957: 245–9), however, offers a different derivation: he traces the term further back, to *Sanoe* and *San sanoe* in Unified Shilla times (668–935 CE).

low-class musicians, was promoted by middle-class locals known as the *chungin*.[12] The ensembles were primarily amateur affairs, and this is indicated by the suffix '*kaek*' that was often used in a group's name to denote a common interest or hobby (*p'ungnyu kaek*, and so on). Low-class musicians were illiterate, so surviving scorebooks were typically compiled by middle-class or aristocratic literati. The *Yuyeji* (Chapter on Artistic Amusement), compiled by Sŏ Yugu (1764–1845) during King Chŏngjo's reign (1776–1800) as part of the intellectual and pragmatic *Sarimp'a* movement, gives *Chul p'ungnyu* repertory information, while specific *Chul p'ungnyu* repertory appear in many other scorebooks, for example, the *Agŭm kobo* (1884), *Chukch'wi kŭmbo* (1890) *Ch'oinmun kŭmbo* (late nineteenth century), and *Samjuk kŭmbo* (1901, with possible earlier roots).

Much of our knowledge of *Chul p'ungnyu* comes from remnants of groups that survived until the recent past. Yi Pohyŏng, who researched these in the 1970s and 1980s, states that professional musicians were often invited to perform alongside amateurs, and that some ensembles described their music as *Samhyŏn yukkak*, a term meaning 'three strings, six instruments' first encountered in respect to a Koryŏ (918–1392) and early Chosŏn dynasty (1392–1910) court ensemble. This ensemble had played 'enjoyable music, tending to be used as an accompaniment to dance' (Chang and Han 1975: 95–6; see also Chang Sahun 1976: 108, 151), but it also had potential associations with shaman ritualists. Hence, the fifteenth-century theorist Pak Yŏn (1378–1458) 'warned his descendants not to let *Samhyŏn yukkak* within the family gates lest it bring about their ruin' (Lee Song-chŏn 1973: 128). Certainly, there are longstanding links between sacred and secular musicians. Equally, many *sanjo* players have also specialized in *Chul p'ungnyu* (for evidence of which, see Kim Chŏngja 1977; Mun 2001).

Kim Ch'angjo's father was a petty official in charge of revenue collection (*hobang*) for Yŏngam County.[13] As a child, Kim proved reluctant to attend the local Confucian academy, where he would have learnt the literary skills necessary to pass civil-service examinations prior to securing appropriate work, but instead preferred to develop his artistic skills. He is reported to have learnt Korean music from the age of seven or eight,[14] and to have first presented a solo *sanjo* performance when 19 years old. Many accounts write that *sanjo* initially met with resistance from the aristocracy. However, it is clear that it quickly won an audience, since we know that other *kayagŭm* musicians began to play it, and in 1896 it was adopted for the *kŏmun'go* six-stringed zither by Paek Nakchun (1876–1934).

The formal characteristics of *sanjo* that remain today emerged with a second generation of performers that included Kim's disciples Han Sŏnggi (1889–1950) and Kim Pyŏngho (1910–1968) – both fellow Yŏngam residents – Ch'oe

---

[12]   There remains confusion about exactly who the *chungin* were, and about who owned and promoted their music in earlier centuries. The musicologist Hahn Man-young's account of *chungin* music (1990: 61–72) sits uncomfortably with the historian Lee Sŏngmu's description (1991: 107–16) of the *chungin* as a group.

[13]   Kim Chukp'a, interviewed by Song Bang-song (Song 1986: 96). See also Kwŏn Tohŭi 2001.

[14]   A 1987 report on *sanjo* issued by the Cultural Properties Research Institute (Munhwajae yŏn'guso) writes that he began to learn music at the age of 10.

Oksam (1901–1956; a student of Chŏng Unyong), Kang T'aehong (1894–1968), An Kiok (1894–1974),[15] An's disciple Chŏng Namhŭi (1910–1984) and, from beyond Chŏlla, Pak Sanggŭn and Shim Sanggŏn.[16] Second-generation musicians contributed the first recordings of *sanjo* as the record industry developed in the 1920s and 1930s,[17] thereby contributing both to the fixing of repertory and to the establishment of specific styles attributed to individual players that are still performed today.[18] Each of these styles is identified as a 'school' after its player. Although the term for 'school', *ryu*, is borrowed from Japan, Korean schools are not equivalent to those of its eastern neighbour. Hence, unlike in Japan, the history of schools remains veiled, part because the second generation of players never wrote down their pieces, but primarily because students expanded and adjusted what they learnt and, indeed, tended to learn from more than one expert teacher.[19] Kim Ch'angjo's *sanjo*, never recorded, has been reconstructed and assessed partly on the basis of second-generation players, notably Han (particularly in an analysis by Mun Chaesuk (2000: 13–30)) and An Kiok. This has led to a considerable industry in its documentation, hence the contemporary performer Yang Sŭnghŭi (2001) has surveyed North Korean publications on Kim's *sanjo*, compiled by, amongst others, An's disciples Chŏng Namhŭi and Kim Chin (b.1926). An also compiled a notation of Kim Ch'angjo's *sanjo* that was reprinted in facsimile in Seoul in 2001 (Kayagŭm sanjo hyŏnjang saŏp ch'ujin wiwŏnhoe, eds, 2001: 335–57). Mun Chaesuk also worked extensively with Kim's granddaughter, Kim Chukp'a (1911–1989), whose *sanjo* school we record here (see, for example, Mun 2000: 30–34).

Of this second generation, all but Shim and Pak were natives of Chŏlla. Because of this, in broad terms at least, the characteristics of Chŏlla music were embedded in *sanjo*, most notably the restricted mode of *kyemyŏnjo*, the slow and highly charged 18/8 rhythmic cycle *chinyangjo*, and considerable melodic ornamentation. These, though, were characteristics not just of shaman rituals, perhaps incorporated through

---

[15] Kim Kwangjun (1886–?) and Chŏng Unyong are mentioned as additional students of Kim Ch'angjo.

[16] Some scholars add additional players to this list, for example Sŏ Kongch'ŏl (Kim Haesuk 1987: 122) and Han Sudong (Han Myŏnghŭi 1985: 435).

[17] A number of SP recordings have been reissued on CD. See, for instance, the five-CD set *Kayagŭm sanjo myŏngindŭl/The Legendary Artists of Korean Kayagŭm Sanjo* (King Records SYNCD-059B – SYNCD-063B, 1993), and *Chŏng Namhŭi, Kayagŭm sanjo ŭi myŏngindŭl 1: Myŏngch'ang Chŏng Namhŭi, Kayagŭm sanjo, Pyŏngch'ang/Kayagum Sanjo, Byung Chang Performed by Nam Hee Chung* (Cantabile SRCD1352, 1996).

[18] Hence, Kim Haesuk (1987) distinguishes seven *kayagŭm sanjo* schools, six of which are associated with second-generation players: Ch'oe Oksam, Shim Sanggŏn, Kim Pyŏngho, Kang T'aehong, Pak Sanggŭn and Sŏ Kongch'ŏl. The seventh is that of Kim Ch'angjo himself, in modern times transmitted through his granddaughter, Kim Chukp'a. Sŏ Kongch'ŏl's school is not common in teaching or performance because of its association with *shinawi*, although in contemporary Korea it has been played and recorded by Kang Chŏngsuk.

[19] A similar concept, *liupai*, exists in China. An interesting panel on 'schools' was held at a Society for Ethnomusicology conference, for which see Siu Wah Yu (2003), Susie Lim (2003) and Philip Flavin (2003).

familiarity with *shinawi* (in some way relating to *shimbanggok*), but also of south-western *minyo* (folksongs) and *p'ansori* (epic storytelling through song). Indeed, the use of rhythmic cycles and the treatment of mode, as we explore in Chapter 4, appears to be influenced primarily by *p'ansori*; musicians and scholars frequently claim that a strong connection exists.[20] Few *sanjo* performers could claim to be competent *p'ansori* singers, so we may surmise that the appeal of *p'ansori* was its success: by the late nineteenth century *p'ansori* was highly prized and popular. By then, singers sought aristocratic patronage and court honours; the aficionado and petty official Shin Chaehyo (1812–1884) encouraged them to introduce literary allusions as he coached them to appeal to higher echelons of society, just as he added literary allusions and smoothed over coarse and low-grade language in collating the texts of extant repertories.[21]

An and Chŏng migrated to North Korea in the late 1940s. For the next 40 years, their names were excised from South Korean accounts of *sanjo*. An spent much of the Korean War period in China, where he taught the Chinese Korean Kim Chin and, following a Chinese directive, was involved in the early work on modernizing the *kayagŭm*. He returned to Pyongyang in 1955, where he was again involved in modernizing the instrument. Kim Chin was also taught by Kim Kwangjun. Chŏng worked at the Pyongyang Music and Dance University until his death, where his most prominent disciple was Kim Killan; he continued to play *sanjo*, though in short rather than extended versions.

In South Korea, a third generation of players proved influential in the years after the Korean War, particularly as *kayagŭm sanjo* was preserved and promoted within the state preservation system. Here a number of holders (*poyuja*) appointed for *kayagŭm sanjo* within Intangible Cultural Property 23 are important. First, Kim Yundŏk (1918–1980) studied with Chŏng Namhŭi and, during the Korean War, with Kang Taehong in the Pusan enclave. To Kim's student Yi Yŏnghŭi (b.1938), in interview in August 1991, the basic form of her teacher's piece, the *pat'ang*, was Chŏng's,[22] but Kim 'added some melodies of Kang and a little more that was his own'.[23] Kim's *sanjo* can be allied to *p'ansori*, and in particular to the masculine and slightly brash 'eastern school' of the vocal genre, from where it takes elements for a number of its integral melodic strands. However, if the foundation of Kim's *sanjo* was Chŏng's style of performance, until 1988 and the beginnings of democracy, this could not be stated in South Korea, so the history was left deliberately vague, forcing the school to be known as Kim Yundŏk's (in, for example, Chaesuk Lee 1971). Second, Sŏng Kŭmyŏn (1923–1986) studied with Pak Sanggŭn and An Kiok; appointed a holder of Property 23 with Kim in 1968, her *sanjo* evolved after she left Chŏlla and settled with her second husband, Chi Yŏnghŭi (1908–1979), a native of the central Kyŏnggi province (Yun Chunggang

---

[20]   Song Bang-song says this, citing his own interviews with prominent *sanjo* musicians and accompanists including Kim Chukp'a, Kim Yundŏk and Kim Myŏnghwan (1987: 84).

[21]   See Chan E. Park (2003: 56–84) for a consideration. Shin's texts were subsequently published (Kang Hanyŏng 1977).

[22]   This is also stated by Chaesuk Lee in '*Kayagŭm ŭi kujo wa chubŏp ŭi pyŏnch'ŏn*' (1998).

[23]   Demonstrated in an analysis by Hee-sun Kim (2000).

and Chŏng Hyŏn'gyŏng 2003). Her association with An was also played down until the late 1980s, but by then she had lost her title as holder after she emigrated with Chi to Hawai'i in 1975. Third, Ham Tongjŏngwŏl (1917–1994; registered name Han Kŭmdŏk) was appointed holder in 1980 for her mastery of the school of Ch'oe Oksam. She was the daughter of a shaman and had trained in Kwangju at a courtesan school, a *kwŏnbŏn*, moving to courtesan institutes in Mokp'o and Wŏnsan. It was only in the latter that at the age of 15 she began her studies with Ch'oe Oksam. Ham talks about her early life in a memoir (1990: 20–25; 32–5). Ch'oe's school is known as the most masculine of all *sanjo* styles, partly because of strident melodies and the use of ornaments encompassing wide intervals. In Ham's performances, her accompanist replaced the normal *changgo* hourglass drum with the *puk* barrel drum. This enhanced the masculine feel because, whereas the hourglass drum uses a light thin stick on the rim of one drum skin and the open hand on the other skin, the barrel drum, commonly used to accompany a *p'ansori* singer, uses a heavy baton to strike both skin and wooden body. The *changgo* is used as the accompanying drum for all other *sanjo* schools. In reality, the barrel drum had little place, but it was introduced by Kim Myŏnghwan (1913–1989), the most famous drum accompanist of recent times. He is reputed to have been Ham's lover in the war years after the couple were displaced from their respective spouses (Chŏng Pŏmt'ae 2002: 248).

Kim Chukp'a

Kim Chukp'a, born on 19 December 1911,[24] was the most important member of the third generation of *sanjo* players. She began to learn to play the *kayagŭm* and literati ensemble music, *p'ungnyu*, from her grandfather, the putative *sanjo* founder Kim Ch'angjo, a year before his death. Her connection to Kim Ch'angjo allows us to gain an impression of what his version of *sanjo* was like. Her father, Kim Nakkwŏn, like Kim Ch'angjo's father, worked for the local government, but Chukp'a's skills were quickly recognized, and she was permitted to enter the Chŏnju Kwŏnbŏn, an institute that trained courtesans, *kisaeng*, normally recruiting from the lower classes. There, she also began to learn *kayagŭm pyŏngch'ang*, a self-accompanied song genre with the zither.

---

[24] By the lunar calendar; in the solar calendar, this would have been at the end of January 1912. In the following paragraphs, ages are given in the Korean reckoning, that is, where a child is considered one year old at birth and gains a year every lunar New Year.

Figure 1.1   Kim Chukp'a

In 1921, at the age of 11, Kim began to train with Han Sŏnggi (1889–1950), her grandfather's disciple. She studied continuously with Han for three years. She became a professional musician when she was 16 years of age, at the time she began working at the Chosŏn Kwŏnbŏn in Seoul, a famous institute that provided skilled girls for artistic functions.[25] She was soon well known, and was given the stage name Kim Unsŏn, meaning 'Angel from the Clouds'. She moved to the Hannam Kwŏnbŏn, also in Seoul, in 1930. A year later, in 1931, she made her first SP record, for O.K. Records, recording *sanjo* and *kayagŭm pyŏngch'ang*. She was invited to Japan to perform, and during the early 1930s gave a number of broadcasts on the Seoul-based radio station Kyŏngsŏng Pangsongguk.[26]

In 1932, at the age of 22, Kim married a man 20 years her senior, the government official Yi Mint'aek. Overnight, as was normal custom, she abandoned her professional career, but Yi liked music and allowed her to continue studying in private. She learnt the six-stringed long zither, *kŏmun'go*, and the literati ensemble music for it, from the well-known master Yi Sŭnghwan. Five years later, in 1937, she began to learn *kŏmun'go sanjo* and the *kagok* lyric song repertory from Ch'oe Pyŏngje. In private, particularly in the house of the wealthy aristocrat Kim Tonggyu, a member of the Andong Kim clan, she played literati ensemble music with others. This continued until 1943, when she was bereaved. She remarried at the age of 34 to Yi Wan'gyu (1891–1977) who, like her first husband, was almost 20 years her senior. He, too, was a government official, and in his later career rose to a senior position within the Ministry of Health. He already had several sons, one of whom had graduated from the prestigious Law Department at the top-ranked Korean university, Seoul National, and later became a public prosecutor. Another son later became a college dean. Yi gave her a new name, Chukp'a, the meaning being a combination of 'bamboo' – a plant known for growing straight and for remaining green throughout the year – and 'fidelity'. At the same time, he registered her[27] under a further name, the very feminine Kim Nanch'o. We do not know her birth name, but from 1943 onwards she was known as Kim Chukp'a. She was now a housewife, largely sequestered within the family compound, and her former life was little more than a distant memory. Yi would not allow her to perform in public, but he, like her first husband, permitted her to study. She learnt a second *kayagŭm sanjo* school from the second-generation musician Shim Sanggon. Kim also taught herself more of *kŏmun'go sanjo*, working from a recording of the master Han Kaptŭk (1919–1987), and is known to have had a few lessons on the seven-stringed bowed zither, *ajaeng*, from Han Ilsŏp (1929–1973), the founder of *ajaeng sanjo*.

In 1950, the Korean War erupted. Kim and her husband escaped the North Korean advance and settled in the south-eastern enclave around Pusan. There, she

---

[25]   Entertainment girls were at the time classified within three grades. The top grade, in which we situate Kim, comprised highly regarded artists and musicians, and did not carry any association with prostitution; this was not the case with the third grade. However, public performance still carried a stigma for women.

[26]   Korean rather than Japanese pronunciations; Kyŏngsŏng rather than Keijō, the Japanese name for colonial Seoul.

[27]   The law required a woman to be registered within her husband's family.

mixed with the wives of many important people who, like her, were sheltering from the fighting. Some wanted to learn *kayagŭm* from her and, because of their high social status, her husband allowed her to begin teaching. Among her first students were a wife of a former prime minister, Chang T'aeksang, the wife of the founder of Korean Air, the wife of the Seoul City mayor, Kim T'aesŏn, and the wife of the influential politician Shin Ikhŭi. By this time, two celebrated *kayagŭm sanjo* performers, Sŏng Kŭmyŏn and Kim Yundŏk, had introduced a new final movement to their *sanjo* pieces. This they called *tanmori*, using a common term taken from *p'ansori*, where it marked a song in a very fast rhythmic cycle. Kim Chukp'a knew the *sanjo* styles of both Sŏng and Kim, and in 1955, after she had returned to Seoul following the end of hostilities, and as she settled back into life as a dutiful wife, she too composed a final section for her own *sanjo*. She called this *sesanjoshi* rather than *tanmori*, probably after a rhythm she knew from the percussion bands of her home district. The fact she chose a different name may have signalled recognition that in her youth she had been more famous than either Sŏng or Kim and, we may presume, she saw no reason to be seen to follow them now.

The scholar Lee Hye-ku, who established the Department of Traditional Music at Seoul National University in 1959, had been a radio presenter in the early 1930s. At that time he had encountered Kim and recognized her formidable musical talent. By the 1960s, after 30 years of marriage, she had been virtually forgotten, but as Chaesuk Lee developed her research on *kayagŭm sanjo* at Seoul National, Lee Hye-ku advised her to seek out Kim Chukp'a as probably the best living performer. So, in December 1967, Chaesuk Lee telephoned Kim's house. She spoke with Kim's husband, Yi Wan'gyu, who was initially reluctant to let his wife teach or talk about music. However, Lee's husband, a businessman, was known to Yi, and Lee herself was by this time a professor at Seoul National University. When Lee explained what she wanted to do, Yi relented, and allowed her to visit. She began to talk with and study from Kim Chukp'a. Lee remembers how Kim remained quiet and humble during her initial visits, subtly revealing the loneliness of being a housewife devoid of any social life and always needing to behave in a way that befitted the Confucian tradition of a dutiful spouse. Lee encouraged her to start teaching other students, and Kim gradually emerged out of her shell, recovering a degree of personal pride at being a knowledgeable musician, the transmitter of Kim Ch'angjo's legacy.

On Christmas Eve 1977, Yi Wan'gyu died. Kim found herself liberated from domestic life; she was finally free to resume her career as a musician. In 1978, she was appointed a holder of Intangible Cultural Property 23 for her *kayagŭm sanjo* skill, in recognition of her importance as the only surviving musician who had studied, albeit briefly, with the putative founder of the genre. She gave her first public performance in her revived career in September 1979, aged 69. She began to perform on radio and TV, and from this time until her death she remained active. She developed her *sanjo*, increasing its total length from 45 to 55 minutes. To do so, she added a seventh *karak* – melodic strand – to the opening *chinyangjo* movement that consisted of 28 complete rhythmic cycles. She added four rhythmic cycles to the *chungjungmori* movement and four to the *chajinmori* movement. In the penultimate movement, *hwimori*, she added 53 rhythmic cycles and extended the free rhythm section at its end, and to the final *sesanjoshi* movement she added seven cycles. She also made slight adjustments to some of the ornamentation that was employed. As she did so, she enabled her students – and scholars thereafter – to trace the evolution of *sanjo* from Kim Ch'angjo forward, and to record it in notation and recordings (compare, for example, Chaesuk Lee 1971: 7–43 and 1983; see also Mun 2000: 37–103). Sadly, Kim Chukp'a died a few days before the harvest festival (*ch'usŏk*) in September 1989.

Other *Sanjo*

Korean scholarship normally considers that *sanjo* was adapted for the six-stringed plucked long zither, *kŏmun'go*, in 1896 by Paek Nakchun (1876–1934). He came from Kanggyŏng in South Ch'ungch'ŏng province, where his father had passed the military service examination. His student, Shin K'waedong (1910–1977), the first holder of Intangible Cultural Property 16, *kŏmun'go sanjo*, once recalled that Paek's father, Paek Sŏndal,[28]

> … used to teach an unknown music to his son with *kuŭm* imitating certain melodies of *p'ansori* or sounds of other instruments. The unknown music turned out later to be the predecessor of today's *kŏmun'go sanjo*. (Song 1986: 98–9)

Kuŭm, literally 'mouth sounds', are verbal onomatopoeia. Assuming Paek's year of birth is correct,[29] his father was senior to Kim Ch'angjo, and it is fascinating to contemplate whether what became *kŏmun'go sanjo* actually preceded Kim Ch'angjo's *kayagŭm sanjo*. This, though, must remain mere contemplation, given a lack of evidence. Shin, born in Iksan in North Chŏlla province, began to learn from Paek in 1926, at the same time as two other students, Kim Chonggi and Pak Sŏkki. Two *sanjo* schools emerged, one through Shim's later student Kim Yŏngjae (b.1947), a current holder of Property 16, and the second from Pak's student Han Kaptŭk (1918–1987).[30]

Towards the end of his life, Shin's playing deteriorated, and a campaign was mounted to remove his appointment and elevate Han to his position.[31] This was successfully countered because Han was junior, but also because of the claim that Han had initially been inspired to learn in 1931 when he heard Pak Chonggi (1879–1939)[32] play a version of *sanjo* for the horizontal bamboo flute, *taegŭm*

---

[28]   Sŏndal is not his given name, but was used by Shin to indicate he had passed the military service examination but had not entered employment in the army.

[29]   There is one Victor SP recording (49055–49057, no date) of Paek Nakchun and a photograph of him, but little verifiable documentation for his life. The dates given here are those of the Cumulative Research Report, number 16 in the series, written by Pak Hŏnbong in 1967. One article by Cho Wimin gives his dates as 1876–1930 (Cho 1969: 22) and a birth date of 1884 has also been suggested.

[30]   A third putative *kŏmun'go sanjo* school is identified by Cho Wimin, that of Kim Yundŏk (Cho 1967, 1969). Kim, though, is better known as a *kayagŭm* player, in which guise we encountered him earlier.

[31]   Kim Kisu, a senior musicologist who had trained in the court music institute during the 1930s, is on record for having raised Shin's competence in meetings of the Cultural Properties Committee.

[32]   There is some dispute about Pak's dates: one source written in his natal home gives his birth as 1880, his last SP recording was made in December 1939 (Regal C2013;

(recounted in Munhwa kongbobu 1985: 319). Han, though, was appointed holder when Shin died, and was duly succeeded after his own death by Shin's student Kim Yŏngjae in 1988. The Intangible Cultural Property was then expanded. Han's school was maintained by his own student, Wŏn Yŏngjae (1922–2002), who was appointed holder in 1993. The one surviving recording of Paek Nakchun has just four movements: the slow 18/8 *chinyangjo*, moderate 12/4 *chungmori*, 5/8+5/8 *ŏnmori* and fast 4/4 *chanmori*. Shin performed a more elaborate piece, with six movements: *chinyangjo*, *chungmori*, moderately fast 12/8 *chungjungmori*, *ŏnmori*, fast 12/8 *chajinmori*, and fast 4/4 *hwimori*.[33] A short note is needed at this point: *kŏmun'go sanjo* was appointed an Intangible Cultural Property before *kayagŭm sanjo*, the former in 1967 and the latter in 1968. The reason for this has nothing to do with *sanjo* as a genre, but reflects the prestige of the *kŏmun'go*, as the favoured zither of the literati (and the instrument for which the bulk of historical scorebooks were written). The six-stringed zither was given precedence in the 1493 treatise *Akhak kwebŏm* (Guide to the Study of Music) over the supposedly indigenous *kayagŭm*. Again, in the twentieth century both Sŏng Kyŏngnin (b.1911) and Chang Sahun (1916–1991), scholars who worked closely with the Cultural Properties Committee and were influential in many Intangible Cultural Property nominations, had trained as *kŏmun'go* performers.

The second CD that accompanies this book, featuring Kim Sunok, is of *kŏmun'go sanjo*. Kim learnt Shin K'waedong's school of *sanjo*, first from Cho Wimin at Seoul National University from 1980 to 1982, and then from 1984 to 1987 from Kim Yŏngjae, who at the time of writing is a professor at the Seoul National University of the Arts. On one of his albums, Kim writes about his studies with Shin:

> I started to learn *kŏmun'go* when I entered the Traditional Music Arts School in 1961 … Two hours were allocated to this as my major every day, and I do not remember thinking little of my *kŏmun'go* class. In my first lesson, I had to spend the day sounding two strings only, the *munhyŏn* and *yuhyŏn*, playing just the sounds known in onomatopoeia as *sal* and *tang*. Not until six months had passed was I allowed to begin to learn the *p'ungnyu* literati ensemble repertory, learning it by heart. My teacher taught me by writing down the onomatopoeia: *tang, tong, ching* and *ching*. My fingers swelled, and the skin of my hand where it rested on the bridge was taken off. My teacher encouraged me. He told me about the instrument and its history, and took me to concerts and radio broadcasts. It was only in my second year of study that I began to learn *kŏmun'go sanjo*.[34]

Moving to the transverse bamboo flute, Pak Chonggi, introduced above, was a musician born in Chindo in the south-west of Chŏlla province who is credited with the development of *taegŭm sanjo*.[35] The report on the basis of which *taegŭm sanjo* was appointed Intangible Cultural Property 45 in 1971, number 68 in the Cumulative

---

issued in 1940), while his name is given for radio broadcasts – and appears in the *Maeil shinbo* newspaper – until July 1941.

[33]   The two versions are transcribed by Song (1986: 245–81).

[34]   Excerpted, with grammar adjusted, from the booklet notes to *Kim Yŏngjae kŏmun'go sanjo, Shin K'waedong ryu/Kim Young-jae's Geomungo Sanjo: Shin Kwe-dong Style* (Synnara Music NSC-078, 2004).

[35]   Stories about Pak, recounted by Chindo islanders in the 1980s, are reported in Howard 1989: 196–8.

series, was authored by the musicologist Kim Kisu (1916–1987). This report identifies a second *taegŭm sanjo* school, that of Kang Paekch'ŏn (1898–1982). A full account of Pak Chonggi and his *sanjo* only recently appeared (Yi Chinwŏn 2007). Whereas Kim writes that Pak's school is based on *p'ansori*, and on particular melodic structures, Kang's is said to derive from the shamanic improvisatory instrumental form, *shinawi*. In fact, Pak throughout his life worked as a shaman ritual musician; his brother's grandson, the shaman and Intangible Cultural Property holder Pak Pyŏngch'ŏn (b.1934), has traced Pak Chonggi's shaman ancestors back eight generations (in Pak Chuŏn and Chŏng Chŏngsu 1988). Initially, though, Kang was appointed holder of Property 45 while Pak's school, transmitted through Han Chuhan and Kwŏn Puja to the popular Yi Saenggang (b.1941), and through Kim Kwangshik to Pak Tonghyŏn and Sŏ Yongsŏk, was not recognized. After Kang's death he was succeeded by his disciple, Kim Tongshik (b.1941), while Yi Saenggang, born in Chŏlla but for many years active in Seoul, was appointed an additional holder in 1996. Yi has recorded widely and is well known for the tremendous fluidity of his playing.

One additional multi-instrumentalist deserves mention at this point: Han Pŏmsu (1911–1984). Han was born in Puyŏ in Ch'ungch'ŏng province and was known for his *sanjo* mastery on two instruments, the *taegŭm* flute and the *haegŭm* two-stringed fiddle. His personal account and notation of *taegŭm sanjo* was published in 1975. As a child he had learnt the two vertical notched flutes, the small *tanso* and larger *t'ungso* (the latter an instrument that in some versions has a sympathetic resonator covering a hole above the finger holes), and he was later associated wth a *sanjo* piece for the *tanso* (Kim Haesuk 1987: 149). He switched to the *taegŭm* horizontal flute in 1929, learning initially from Kim Tup'al, and at the same time taking up the fiddle. He heard Pak Chonggi on the radio and determined to learn *taegŭm sanjo* from him, so in 1935 moved to Seoul, where Pak was living, to do so (Chŏng Pŏmt'ae 2002: 196–200); he also worked with Kim Tongshik, Kang Paekch'ŏn's disciple (Yi Chinwŏn 2007: 87). A *sanjo* piece also exists for a further flute, the end-blown *t'ungso*, and it has been suggested that this was devised by Yu Tongch'o (1881–1946), based on Han's *taegŭm sanjo*. The *t'ungso sanjo* was performed and recorded at the National Center for Korean Traditional Performing Arts in July 1956 by Kim Sanghŭi. Yu, however, like Han in his youth, was primarily a *tanso* performer, and his recording of *tanso sanjo*, on Victor Star KS–2007, accompanied by Han Sŏngjun on drum, survives;[36] this has been analysed by Yi Chinwŏn (2004: 253–80).

Chi Yonggu (1862–?) is generally considered to have first developed a version of *sanjo* for the two-stringed fiddle, *haegŭm*.[37] The fiddle dates in Korea back to at least the eleventh century, and in its construction it uniquely once included all eight materials of the Chinese material schema – a bamboo resonator and neck, wooden pegs, rosin (earth), a metal base plate and spike, silk strings, a gourd bridge, leather on the bow, and a coating of crushed stone inside the resonator. *Sanjo* for the fiddle moves us away from the south-western Chŏlla provinces to the central Kyŏnggi province, and from the widely reported influence of *p'ansori* towards

---

[36]   A reel tape also exists, held by the Korean Culture and Arts Foundation (Han'guk Munhwa Yesul Chinhŭngwŏn) (catalogue number AT304).

[37]   See Yu Kiryong and Hong Yunshik (1968: 122).

musicians who made their living partly or substantially from providing instrumental accompaniments for shaman rituals local to Kyŏnggi. Chi's *sanjo* was inherited by Chi Yŏnghŭi, the husband of the *kayagŭm sanjo* maestro Sŏng Kŭmyŏn. Chi's *sanjo* is lighter in atmosphere than *kayagŭm sanjo* or *kŏmun'go sanjo*, with little of the south-western sorrowful mode and emotional ornamentation, and much more that is dance-like, in particular a movement in the 6/8+6/8 *kutkŏri* rhythmic cycle. The influence of Kyŏnggi shaman rituals is seen in the use of a medium-paced 6/4 ritual rhythmic cycle, *ŏtchungmori*. However, Han Pŏmsu's *haegŭm sanjo* also survives, remaining more faithful to the south-western tradition.[38] The two schools, of Chi and Han, increased in popularity in the 1960s,[39] and since then two additional schools have evolved, by Sŏ Yongsŏk and Kim Yŏngjae, the former maestro known primarily as a *taegŭm* specialist and the latter as a *kŏmun'go* player. Sŏ makes greater use of the south-western *kyemyŏnjo* mode, while Kim, in essence, arranges melodies from a diverse palette and at times indulges in composition, particularly in two fast movements, the 5/8+5/8 *ŏnmori* and 12/8 *hwimori*, where he is concerned with motivic development and sectional contrast. So, today, four *haegŭm sanjo* schools exist, and all four are recorded on a single album, *Pak Chongshil Haegŭm sanjo yuram/The Haegŭm Sanjo of Four Ryu* (Top TOPCD-014, 1999).

Sanjo for the Korean oboe, *p'iri*, developed with Yi Ch'ungsŏn and Ch'oe Ŭngnae, the former being the teacher of one of today's most respected players, Chŏng Chaeguk (b.1942) (Song Pangsong 1984: 555); a further *p'iri sanjo* school is now identified with the composer and performer Pak Pŏmhun (b.1948), a nephew of the *kayagŭm sanjo* master Ham Tongjŏngwŏl. Versions for the bowed zither, *ajaeng*, and the shawm, *soaenap*, also appeared after 1945. *Ajaeng sanjo* was initially associated with Han Ilsŏp (1929–1973) and the first known performance was in 1948; Pak Chongsŏn (b.1941) is a well-known contemporary player (Kim Haesuk 1987: 129–30). Finally, although such is the popularity of *sanjo* today that it is likely to continue evolving in future years, we should mention *sanjo* for the hourglass-shaped double-headed drum, *changgo*, which Kim Duk Soo (b.1952) premiered at the start of the new millennium.[40]

---

[38] For which, see Song Kwŏnjun (1984).

[39] See Chu Yŏngwi (2004: 367–408) for a comparative analysis.

[40] Howard recently suggested in his *Creating Korean Music* that the 1982 solo drum piece Kim and his colleagues devised for the percussion quartet SamulNori was influenced by *sanjo* as much as by the solo drum pieces of rural percussion bands (2006: 51–2).

Chapter 2

The Instrument: *Kayagŭm*

The *kayagŭm*, the instrument that we are primarily concerned with in this volume, is a 12-stringed half-tube zither or long zither that organologists, following the Hornbostel and Sachs classification system, would code as 312.22.5.[1] It resembles the Chinese *zheng*, the Mongolian *yatga*, the Japanese *koto* and the Vietnamese *dan tranh*. In the 1493 *Akhak kwebŏm* (Guide to the Study of Music), the *kayagŭm* is labelled as an indigenous Korean instrument while a second Korean zither, the six-stringed *kŏmun'go*, is depicted as having Chinese antecedents. This led to the *kayagŭm* disappearing from most court ensembles, particularly ritual ensembles, while the *kŏmun'go* remained the favoured instrument of literati. The *zheng* also decreased in prominence in Chinese court ensembles from the Ming dynasty onwards (Liang 1984: 893) but, in contrast to both Korean and Chinese zithers, the *koto* remained almost exclusively a court instrument in *gagaku* ensembles until Kenjun (1547–1636) and Yatsuhashi Kengyō (1614–1684) adopted it to provide song accompaniments (Kaufmann 1976: 100; Kishibe 1982: 55–6). The *yatga*, although it had since the fourteenth century possessed 13 strings in contrast to the 12 of the *kayagŭm*, was revived in the early 1930s on the basis of Korean instruments; this has now become core to Buryat ensembles across the border in the Russian Federation.[2]

In Korea, two distinct versions of the traditional *kayagŭm* survive. The larger, associated with court and literati ensembles, is known as the *pŏpkŭm, p'ungnyu kayagŭm* or *chŏngak kayagŭm* (*pŏp* = law; *p'ungnyu* = elegant music; *chŏngak* = 'upright music' or 'correct music'). This has a body made from a single piece of paulownia wood (*odong namu*). The wood is cut from a plant between 30 and 60 years old; older wood is considered too solid and younger wood too soft to produce adequate resonance. Although more than ten sub-species of paulownia are known in East Asia, Korean

---

[1]   This classification system dates from 1914. Recent interpretations are by Jairazhboy (1990) and Dournon (1992).

[2]   See Dorchieva (2006). In addition, below we mention *se* and *zhu* zithers. The bamboo element, seen in the Chinese character used to write their name, is also present in the character for *zheng*, which suggests common roots. We can trace *zheng* back to Qin times (897–221 BCE). A second element in the character, 'quarrel', introduces a legend, in which two brothers quarrelled over an instrument and split it in two, one with 12 strings and the second with 13. The brothers were sisters, and one migrated to Korea with the 12-stringed instrument, according to Adriaansz (1973). A similar legend is known in Vietnam. In China, both 12-stringed and 13-stringed *zheng* have been used. Today, and in respect to the known history, the *koto* typically has 13 strings and the *kayagŭm* 12. In Mongolia there is a splendid and distinct legend that tells how Queen Agai Shabdal played, with understandable difficulty, an instrument with a mere 8,000 strings. Connections appear to indicate intercultural exchange across the region. See Van Gulik 1951: 13; Crossley-Holland 1959: 238; Tran Van Khe 1967: 85–6; Adriaansz 1973; Liang 1984: 893; Nixon 1984: 884; Howard 1988: 169–70.

wood is preferred over Japanese and Chinese varieties, cut from high in the mountains just below the tree line, normally from rocky areas such as Sŏrak, Chiri and Songni mountains. The density of the wood is said to generate the round but slightly damped sound of a finished instrument. Good craftsmen sort through several dozen pieces of wood before choosing one they consider suitable. Planks are cut to 160–170 cm lengths and weathered for a minimum of three years, during which time they are monitored to prevent cracking and warping. A slightly convex front is fashioned by planing along the grain. The soundbox is hollowed out by hand through a large rectangular opening at the back, while the back remains flat. The thickness of the soundboard is determined by touch, and touch is considered the most critical part of a maker's skill. Finally, the soundboard is scorched with an iron to enhance the grain and to burn off resin.

Strings are made from wound silk between 200-ply and 400-ply in thickness, typically bought at country markets in spring and autumn and boiled for just the right amount of time to remove starch but retain flexibility. Above a fixed hardwood bridge (*hyŏnch'im*; lit., 'string pillow') the strings pass through holes drilled from the front to the back of the instrument, where they are held by pegs (*tolgwae*). Below the fixed bridge, strings pass over movable bridges (*anjok*) typically made from jujube or cherry wood that define the sounding length. Because of their shape, the movable bridges are often referred to as 'wild geese feet' (*kirogi pal*) and have inset cuts at their apex for the string and slightly curved bases to their two feet that allow them to flex in relation to the soundboard when a string is stretched. Bridges come in sets, joined together by a thread decorated at its ends with knot tassels (*maedŭp*). Bridges and strings are changed every two or three years, and professional musicians cut fresh lengths of strings a day or so before a performance. Spare string is coiled at the lower end of the soundboard. The coils are held behind loops of coloured cords known as *haksul* after the knee of a crane. These are in turn attached to the top end of blue, brown or red cords (*pudŭl*) that are secured by passing around and through a red sandalwood extension to the instrument's body known as the 'ram's horns' (*yangidu*). There is no knot to keep the strings tensioned but, rather, the cords are doubled back on themselves to harness friction. For aesthetic appearance, the cords are then bundled together in a decorative figure '8', with the top and bottom of this figure tucking under the cords near the loops.

In August 1990, Ko Hŭnggon (b.1951), one of today's finest zither makers, remarked to Howard:

> I build instruments just like in the past. I study the old ways of doing things and scour the country to find proper materials. Korean string instruments have a particular tone colour, a specific smell (*hyang*). Today, we can once more use really old production methods because we have ancient instruments and old records detailing how instruments were played. We know how they were made back in Shilla times [traditional dates 57 BCE – 935 CE]. Koreans now want to preserve the old. Performers see little need to change anything, although we have cleaned up and improved the sounds that instruments make and smartened their look. The right way forward is to preserve traditional forms and to keep instruments just as we have inherited them.

The second instrument, now called the *sanjo kayagŭm* after the folk-art genre that we explore in this book, has a shorter and narrower body with a planed and scorched paulownia soundboard married to sides and back of a harder wood such as chestnut. Makers buy hardwood direct from merchants. Since the construction alleviates the need to hollow out the soundbox, the backpiece typically has three soundholes: the new moon (*ch'osaeng tal*) above the Chinese character for happiness (*hŭi* in Sino-Korean) given as a decorated oblong, and the full moon (*porŭm tal*). Some old instruments have calligraphy or engraved inscriptions. Ivory or plastic strips cover joints, and an elaborate inlay of wood or bone may fill the area above the fixed bridge. Only an echo of ram's horns survives, again carved from a separate piece of hardwood but now described as the 'phoenix tail' (*pongmi*).[3] The *sanjo kayagŭm* probably developed in the nineteenth century to facilitate the rapid flurries required by folk musicians (Yi Hyegu 1976: 19; Rockwell 1974: 35). Although some associate it with Kim Ch'angjo, it may actually predate the introduction of the *sanjo* genre, not least since it is more portable than the large instrument and would consequently have been useful for travelling musicians, including shaman ritualists.[4] Even if it developed as late as the nineteenth century, models for its construction, with separate sides and back, existed many centuries before in the Korean *kŏmun'go* and *ajaeng* zithers and in the Chinese *zheng*.

The Historical Record

The written record of the *kayagŭm* begins with *Samguk sagi* (History of the Three Kingdoms), compiled by Kim Pushik in the twelfth century. In one section, dealing with the twelfth and thirteenth years (551–552) of the chronicles of King Chinhŭng (r.540–576) of the south-eastern Shilla kingdom, we are told how King Kashil, ruler of the Kaya confederation, heard a Chinese *zheng* and commented that since countries do not share languages they should not have the same music. U Rŭk, a musician from Sŏngyŏl prefecture, was ordered to create a new instrument and compose for it. He did so, leaving the names of 12 pieces that suggest the appropriation of local folksongs: *Hagarado, Sanggarado, Pogi, Talgi, Samul, Mulhye, Hagimul, Sajagi, Kŏyŏl, Sap'alhye, Isa* and *Sanggimul*. In 551, U Rŭk fled with his student Yi Mun (the composer of three pieces named after rats, crows and quails) to Shilla, where Chinhŭng allowed him to settle in Kugwŏn (now Ch'ungju in North Ch'ungch'ŏng province). A year later the king sent *taenama* Pŏpchi and Kyego and *taesa* Mandŏk to learn his music.[5] They considered it unrefined, so reconstructed the 12 melodies as five works suitable for Shilla court use. This distanced the music from its roots, and *Samguk sagi* tells how 'treacherous' officials argued that music from an overrun federation should not be preserved. It is said that U Rŭk's anger at the revisions turned to tears of joy when he heard the new pieces performed.

We have cited this legend from Kim Tonguk's Korean modern translation in *Kaya munhak* (Cultural Literature of Kaya; 1966);[6] the legend is repeated in a number of musicological essays (for example, Kwŏn 1985: 93). There are, though, three potential

---

    [3]   Feet, tongues and more dragon and phoenix ephemera are associated with both the Korean six-stringed *kŏmun'go* zither (Howard 1988) and with the Japanese *koto* (Johnson 2004).
    [4]   Note, though, that the courtesan instrument painted by Shin Yunbok at the end of the eighteenth century (see below) is the court version with distinct 'ram's horns'.
    [5]   *Taenama* is the official title for the tenth degree of the Shilla 17 ranks and *taesa* refers to the twelfth degree.
    [6]   The original is in volume (*kwŏn*) 32.8a2–b2 of *Samguk sagi*.

problems with the legend. First, it seems to contrast the way that the instrument is depicted in artefacts that predate Chinhŭng's time. Second, complex instruments are typically given high value in pre-industrial societies and it seems unlikely that U Rŭk would have found it easy to flee to a rival kingdom with what we must assume was the prized *kayagŭm*. Third, Kashil is not mentioned in any other historical document.[7]

Chen Suo's (233–297) *Sanguo zhi* (History of Three Kingdoms) states that Koreans in the south of the peninsula, in the area later consolidated by the Kaya Federation[8] used a '*se* (K: *sŭl*) that was not a *zhub*[9] (K: *ch'uk*)' (vol.30.42b5; Kwŏn 1985: 92). The instrument was plucked, and specific musical pieces for it are thought to have existed. The later Korean text *Samguk sagi* also indicates – though we should remember that it was written a long time after the events and that no other surviving written record corroborates it – that the musician Mulgyeja played the *qin* (K: *kŭm*) and composed pieces for it during the reign of King Naehae (r.196–230 CE), while Paekkyŏl, a musician during the reign of King Chabi (r.458–479), played the *qin* to produce a rice-pounding sound he titled '*Taeak*'. The Chinese *qin* is a seven-stringed long zither without bridges that in construction is distant from the *kayagŭm*. Korean scholars, on the basis of the comment that '*qin* in Korean means *ko*' in the 1527 *Hunmong chahoe*, a textbook for Chinese character learning, argue that '*qin/kŭm*' must denote an indigenous instrument (Song Pangsong 1984: 39–40; Kwŏn Osŏng 1985). The character *qin*, in Korean pronunciation *kŭm*, then, is interpreted as a loan word appropriated to write the purely Korean '*ko*' before the introduction of a Korean alphabet.[10]

The archaeological record offers glimpses of an even longer history. Vestiges of ancient wooden zithers were discovered in Shinch'ang-dong, Kwangju city, and in the Imdang housing development area of Kyŏngsan city in 1997 and 1998 respectively. They are 77–79 cm long and at the most 28 cm wide, and have been dated to between the first century BCE and the first century CE (one is depicted in Figure 2.1). Could these be prototypes for the *kayagŭm*? Press reports in the *Chosŏn ilbo* (*Korean Daily News*; 19 July 1997 and 10 June 1998) suggest so. Beyond the main body a neck projects, as if this was where the 'ram's horns' were once attached. These horns are a primary characteristic of the *kayagŭm*, clearly distinguishing it from other East Asian zithers. The horns are depicted in two early terracotta figurines (*t'ou*). The first, not illustrated here, has been dated to the reign of King Mich'u (r.261–284) and is of a headless torso carrying the zither (the first picture of this was printed in Lee Hye-Ku 1957: 367). The second figure, from a later era (Pratt 1987: 237–8), performs on the instrument and is moulded on a long-necked vase discovered in Hwangnam-dong, Kyŏngju city, in 1974 (Figure 2.2). This is currently owned by the National Museum. The neck of the jar incorporates other animals, and the figure playing the zither is a pregnant woman, so an inference may be made that the zither was used in some form of fertility rite. The crude execution indicates six strings rather than today's 12, but we should be wary of considering such figurines as faithful reproductions.

---

[7]   One 'Kasul' is, however, found in a Japanese source, who might be the same ruler (Kwŏn 1985: 90).

[8]   The characters defining place used by Chen Suo transliterate as 'Pyŏnjin' in Korean, which is a combination of the names of two earlier states, Pyŏn (?–42 CE) and Chin (?–57 CE).

[9]   Koreans musicologists describe the *zhu/ch'uk* as a 13-stringed zither similar in construction to the *qin* (K: *kŭm*) (for example Chang 1984: 745).

[10]   The musicologist Chang Sahun thus combines the two, describing the '*kogŭm*' (1984: 95 and 1969: 77); this though is in a discussion primarily about a different zither, the six-stringed *kŏmun'go*.

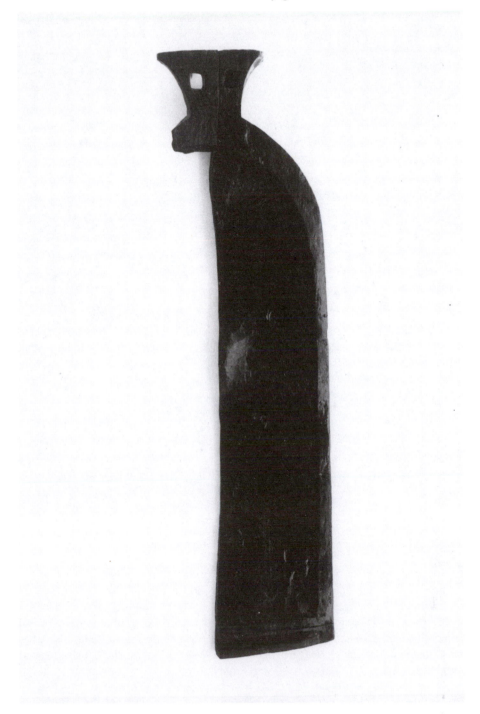

Figure 2.1   An early wooden zither, presumed to be a precursor to the *kayagŭm*

Figure 2.2 Vase excavated at Kyŏngju, showing a zither

Both terracotta zither representations have prominent 'ram's horns': this is the primary feature that demonstrates a consistent form for the instrument from early times through to the present day (Kim Ujin 1989: 92). One of the figurines also has a cord hooked to the side of the instrument. This cord is not visible in more recent depictions of the *kayagŭm*, neither in the 1848 *Chinch'an ŭigwe* (Court Writings on Chinch'an Banquets) (Hayashi Kenzō 1984: 136), nor in the illustrations of instruments in the 1493 *Akhak kwebŏm* (Guide to the Study of Music). Volume seven of *Akhak kwebŏm* (Yi Hyegu 1979, 2: 136–41) records the structure of the *kayagŭm* in great detail, with drawings (Figure 2.3) and precise measurements. It records that the body, right to the horns, should be made from a single piece of wood, although contemporary instruments use a separate piece of harder wood for the horns. The horns are depicted curving outwards, as if an ox's horns, rather than those of a sheep that are customary today. Going further back in time, the cord is present along with horns in two ninth-century *shiragi koto* (J. for 'Shilla *kayagŭm*') preserved in almost perfect shape at the Shōsōin repository in Nara, Japan (Figure 2.4).[11] Song Pangsong claims that the zither that appears in ninth-century Japanese literature such as the *Nihon kōki* (Postscript of Japan) and the *Koji ruian* (Ancient Garden) is the Korean *kayagŭm* rather than Japanese *koto* (1984: 83). Whereas a typical court *kayagŭm* is now almost 167 cm in length and 28.5 cm in width, surviving historical instruments are shorter but wider; the Shōsōin instruments measure 158.1 cm and 153.3 cm in length by 30.9 cm and 30.5 cm wide respectively, while *Akhak kwebŏm* gives a measurement of 157.6 cm by 31.5 cm (Kenzō 1964; Hwang Pyŏngju 1990: 39–40).

No *kayagŭm* appears in the early tomb paintings from the northern Korean kingdom of Koguryŏ (traditional dates 37 BCE – 668 CE) that have been excavated in present-day North Korea and China. The tombs containing paintings of musical activity – Anak Tomb 3, the Tomb of the Dancers at Tongguo, and Changchuan Tomb 1 – date from the late fourth century onwards and depict the now defunct *ohyŏn*, a five-stringed vertical fretted lute that is associated with the *kŏmun'go* six-stringed fretted zither.[12] A millennium later, a surviving genre painting by Shin Yunbok (1758–?; pen-name Hyewŏn) is one of very few depictions of the *kayagŭm*. Titled 'Picnic by the Lotus Pond', this is part of a set of illustrations that challenged the norms of aristocratic lifestyles. It depicts a courtesan playing the zither for male clients (Figure 2.5). This indicates something of the *kayagŭm*'s fortunes. Back in the seventh century when the Korean peninsula was united under Unified Shilla, the five revised pieces by U Rŭk's disciples became associated with the *Samhyŏn samjuk* ensemble of three stringed instruments (*kayagŭm*, *kŏmun'go*, *pip'a* lute) and three bamboo flutes (big *taegŭm*, medium *chunggŭm* and small *sogŭm*). The ensemble, and perhaps the repertory, survived through the Koryŏ dynasty (918–1392)[13] and the first century of the Chosŏn dynasty, until King Sŏngjong's reign (r.1469–1494) (Chang 1969: 79–80).

As the state adopted Confucianism in later Koryŏ and early Chosŏn times, however, court music was codified, separating esteemed Chinese imports from lesser indigenous repertories. The *kayagŭm* was associated with the local, possibly because its name implied a Korean invention. Thus, in the *Akhak kwebŏm*, it is discussed after other zithers, implying a lower ranking. From then onwards it occupied a position of constantly shifting importance. It was dropped from state rituals in 1593, and thereafter moved in and out of court ensembles. While many scorebooks remain for the literati-favoured *kŏmun'go*, only a handful survive for the *kayagŭm*. Indeed, the earliest *kayagŭm* score, the 1796

---

[11]   The two are named, in Korean transliteration, as *kŭmbagap shillagŭm* and *kŭmni shillagŭm*. The repository also has a further badly damaged instrument and the vestige of a further wooden ram's horn (Hayashi Kenzō 1964: 38–40).

[12]   See Song (1991) for illustrations. Song applies considerable detective skills in his attempt to trace the development of Koguryŏ instruments, and in an earlier account (Song 1986) offers the most complete historical picture for the *kŏmun'go* published to date in English.

[13]   As is confirmed by *Samguk sagi* (vol. 32.5b6–9) and *Koryŏsa* (History of the Koryŏ Dynasty; 1452) (vol. 71.30b8, 31a2).

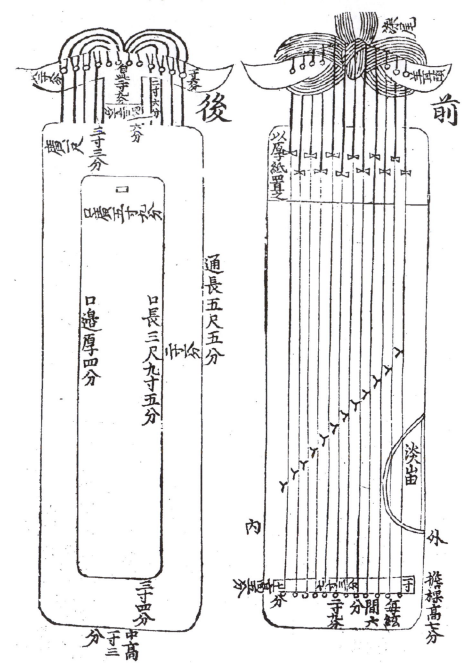

Figure 2.3   The *kayagŭm*, as depicted in *Akhak kwebŏm*

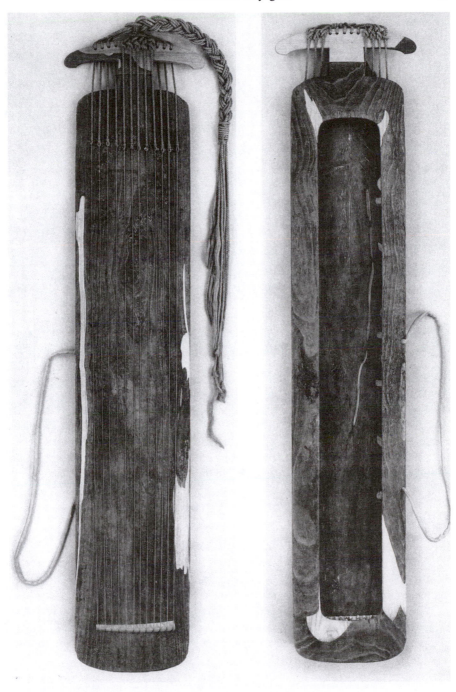

Figure 2.4   A *shiragi koto* from the Shōsōin repository

Figure 2.5   'Picnic by the Lotus Pond' by Shin Yunbok (1758–?)

Choljang mannok, has yet to be fully deciphered.[14] Although Rockwell (1974) states that the names now associated with the larger zither version, 'elegant zither' (*p'ungnyu kayagŭm*) and 'zither of the law' (*pŏpkŭm*), were consciously adopted in efforts to raise its status, a hint of ambivalence remains, since Korean musicians typically still today consider the *kŏmun'go* a man's instrument but the *kayagŭm* a woman's.

Performance Techniques

Right-hand *kayagŭm* techniques include plucking, pushing and flicking strings. The left hand, working below the movable bridges, adjusts the pitch and adds ornaments as a string is sounded by pushing a string to raise its pitch, pulling to lower its pitch, and providing vibrato by a repeated push and release tremolo.

Techniques for the court instrument have been modified over time, as is demonstrated by a comparison of scorebooks, starting with the *Choljang mannok* and progressing through the 1913 *Kungnip kugagwŏnbo* (Court music institute score)

---

[14]   This score is also known as the *Chorong kayagŭmbo*. The compilation date is given as the twentieth year of King Chŏngjo's reign – that is, 1796. Chang Sahun has published a reasonably detailed but still incomplete account of the score (Chang 1983: 295–300) and also provided an introduction to a facsimile of the score published in *Han'guk ŭmakhak ch'ongsŏ charyo* 16: 20–23 and 151–61 (Kungnip kugagwŏn 1984).

archived at the National Center for Korean Traditional Performing Arts, the 1916 *Pangsanhanssi kŭmbo* (Han of Pangsan's string score) to an anonymous 1930s score. Right-hand striking techniques are usually gentle: pushing a string with the soft part of the forefinger to pluck it rather than plucking with the nail, adding occasional flicks.[15] Formulaic ornament techniques are used: the left hand adds light vibrato (*nonghyŏn*) that increases in frequency as a pitch continues over time, but the pitch *chung* (today, aᵇ) is played without vibrato; one string is pulled to create a major second melodic descent when repeating the note *im* (today, bᵇ) in the *kyemyŏnjo* mode; phrases may commence with two low acciaccature (*sŭlgidŭng*) or a single acciaccatura a fifth below (*ssareng*); a string can be pushed to tighten it and raise the pitch by a perfect fourth, and so on.

The *sanjo kayagŭm* uses more varied right-hand techniques including double flicks and, to allow for rapid passagework, more finger variation, concentrating on the thumb, index and middle finger. The techniques can be divided into two types: basic, single-strike techniques (in our brief discussion here it should be kept in mind that basic forms taught and mastered during training undergo modification in performance), and combination techniques comprising two strikes within a single unit. The basic right-hand techniques are:

- *plucking with the index finger* (Figure 2.6)
  The thumb is placed against the first joint of the index finger to support it. Both fingers should be relatively relaxed, with the side of the hand behind the little finger resting on the instrument above the bridge. The remaining fingers rest on strings below and adjacent to the string to be plucked. The string is plucked in an inward and upward motion, the wrist rotating. When strings are plucked in ascending sequences, the middle finger damps the string as the index finger plucks the next string; in descending sequences, the thumb damps the string as the next is plucked.
- *flicking with the index finger* (Figure 2.7)
  The starting position is to make a circle: the nail of the index finger is held against the soft part of the thumb in front of the first joint. The thumb is placed on the string above the one to be sounded, pushing the string downwards with slight pressure, while the side of the hand remains in contact with the instrument above the bridge. The flick is accomplished by creating a circular motion of the index finger.
- *plucking with the middle finger*
  Used to play pitches typically an octave below the main melody. The side of the hand remains in contact with the instrument above the bridge, but the fourth and little fingers do not rest on lower strings, there is no connection between middle finger and thumb, and less rotation of the wrist is employed.
- *plucking with the thumb* (Figure 2.8)
  The thumb plucks upwards and outwards; the side of the hand remains in contact with the instrument above the bridge. In the most basic form, index,

---

[15] For discussions of zither techniques based on court music repertory see Howard (1988: 180–84, in English) or Sŏng Shimon (1987: 18–23, in Korean). A more recent account that divides court techniques from *sanjo* and contemporary techniques is Jae-kyung Lee (2003: 29–46).

middle, fourth and little fingers rest on lower strings, but the index finger will typically rest on the next string to be plucked (rather than always on the string immediately below the string plucked by the thumb).

The combination techniques comprise:

- *a double flick with the index and middle fingers*
  Typically used in the faster-paced movements of *sanjo* (in the case of Kim Chukp'a's *sanjo*, in the *hwimori* and *sesanjoshi* movements). The index finger is held against the thumb, and the thumb pushes slightly down on the string above those to be sounded, as with the single flick. The middle finger is placed behind and below the first joint of the index finger; there should be little space between index and middle finger at their second joint. The little finger, but not the fourth finger, normally rests on a lower-pitched string or on the bridge of the instrument. The middle finger flicks first, then the index finger, each creating a circular motion that ends close to the horizontal at roughly the same level as the fourth finger.
- *push and pluck with the index finger and thumb*
  Sounding pairs of strings less than an octave and normally two pentatonic pitches distant to each other, this technique is used in ascending and descending sequences. Using the *kayagŭm* tuning for Kim Chukp'a's *sanjo*, the sequences would typically be G–d, c–g, d–a, g–c' and so on ascending, and c'–g, a–d, g–c, d–G descending. In ascending sequences, the index finger pushes the lower-pitched string then, as the thumb plucks the upper-pitched string, the first string is damped by the middle finger. Descending, the thumb goes first, followed by the index finger plucking the lower-pitched string. In this description, we use 'push' ('drag' is preferred in some texts) to indicate that the thumb/finger does not inscribe any upward circular motion.
- *pluck and pluck with the middle finger and thumb*
  Sounding pairs of strings usually an octave or more apart, again in ascending (for example, G–g, c–c', d–d', g–g', a–a', and so on) and descending sequences (for example, a'–a, g'–g, d'–d, and so on). Ascending, the thumb plucks the higher pitched string first, followed by the middle finger plucking the lower-pitched string. Descending, the middle finger goes first. Both fingers pluck in a circular, upward motion; the middle finger does not come to rest on an adjacent string.
- *push and pluck with the index finger*
  Two ascending pitches on adjacent strings are sounded by the index finger. The first string is pushed, the index finger coming to momentary rest on the second string, then the middle finger damps the first string as the second is plucked in the basic upward and outward motion.
- *push and push with the thumb*
  Two descending pitches on adjacent strings sounded by the thumb. The first is pushed, the thumb coming to rest on the second string, then the second is pushed – rather than plucking in the basic upward motion, it is normal to push the thumb forward and down.

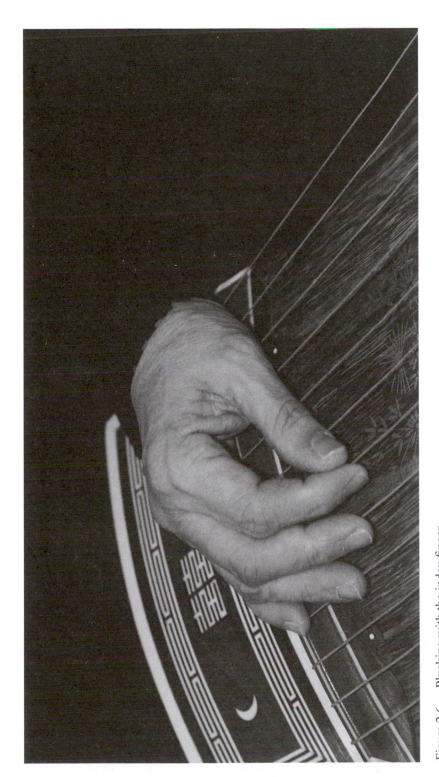

Figure 2.6   Plucking with the index finger

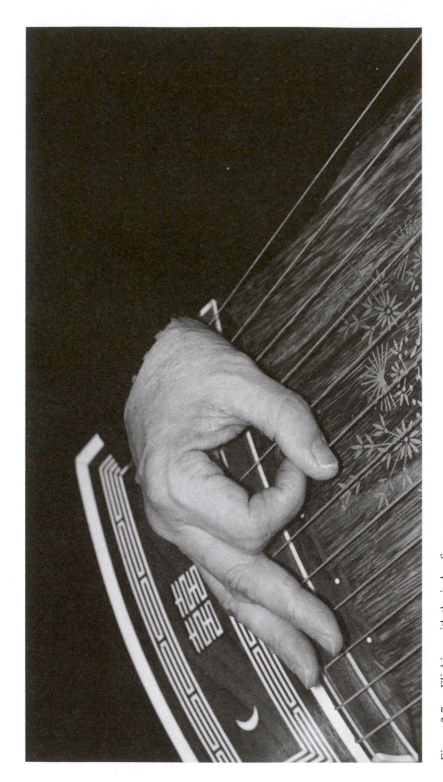

Figure 2.7   Flicking with the index finger

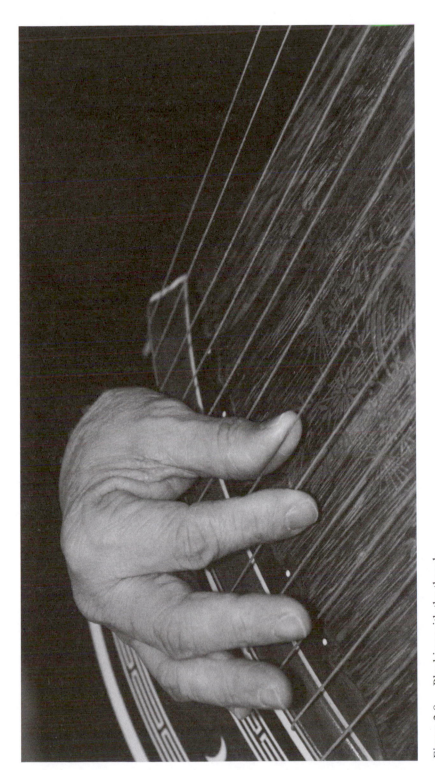

Figure 2.8　Plucking with the thumb

Ornaments are more fluid in *sanjo* than in the court repertory. Vibrato is deeper and more rapid, beginning as soon as a tone sounds, but respects modal characteristics and the functions of specific tones in particular modes (as we will see in Chapter 4). The after-tone is important and incorporates pushing and pulling techniques that lower and raise the pitch as the sound envelope progresses. Use can be made of pitches outside those pre-tuned on the instrument, normally created by pushing a string to the left of the movable bridge to raise its pitch by a tone or more. Table 2.1 lists ornament and technique symbols used in the notation below.

Table 2.1   Ornament and Finger Technique Symbols

➉   play on string nominally pitched one tone below by pulling to lower pitch (LH)

➊   play on string nominally pitched one tone lower by pushing to raise pitch (LH)

ﾉﾄ   no vibrato

丂   *chŏnsŏng*: after striking, pull string to lower pitch then release (LH)

⋀   push string quickly after striking to raise pitch then release (LH)

╱   after string is plucked, push string gradually to give rising glissando (LH)

╲   after string is plucked, pull string gradually to give falling glissando (LH)

╰   portamento from above: push before string is plucked then release (LH)

╲   falling portamento: pull string after plucking (LH)

ᙏᙏ   vibrato; push and release string repeatedly (LH); can combine with glissando

Cᙏᙏ   wide vibrato (LH)

○   flick string, rather than pluck, with index finger (RH)

8   flick string with middle finger (RH)

NB: This is an abbreviated table, giving only those symbols used in the *sanjo* notation below.[1]

---

[1]   For a discussion of ornaments, see Howard (1988).

While the division of labour between the two hands – right-hand fingers for plucking strings, left-hand fingers for adding ornaments and pitch alteration – is maintained on both court and *sanjo* instruments, additional techniques have been exploited in contemporary compositions that are played on the *sanjo kayagŭm* and on modified instruments. These techniques include using the left hand to the right of the bridges to contribute melodic lines and harmonic accompaniment, incorporating arpeggios played by either or both hands, distinguishing staccato and legato, damping strings to create a *con sordini* effect, sounding harmonics by partially stopping strings at nodes, playing glissandi to the left of the bridges, scratching strings with finger nails, tremolo effects, percussive knocking on the wooden soundboard, and so on.

New *Kayagŭm*

The two traditional *kayagŭm* are no longer alone. An Kiok, the *kayagŭm sanjo* maestro who moved to North Korea in the late 1940s, spent the Korean War years in Yanji (K: Yŏnbyŏn) in China's Jilin province. It was there, under a directive from the communist regime, that work on an 'improved' (*kaeryang*) zither began in 1953; the Yanji-based scholar Kim Tŭkkyun remembers that Shin Hanim, a Korean who had studied in the Soviet Union, was closely involved with this work.[16] Back in Pyongyang from 1955, An continued this work, prior to the 1960 establishment of a North Korean instrument committee. A 21-stringed instrument was the result, with metal tuning pegs and nylon strings. The instrument has separate folding legs, to allow it to be played seated rather than, as with traditional court and *sanjo* versions, on the floor. A box at the lower end encloses pegs, replacing the 'ram's horns'. The instrument keeps the overall range of the *sanjo kayagŭm*, but fills in missing diatonic pitches to accommodate Western soundworlds. The nylon strings are less flexible than the silk strings of traditional instruments, and although vibrato is retained many pre-tone and post-tone ornaments have been dropped. In South Korea, modification began in the 1960s – we prefer the term *pyŏn'gyŏng* or *kaejo* ('to modify') rather than *kaeryang* ('to improve'). Executed or supported by the National Center for Korean Traditional Performing Arts (for which see Mun Hyŏn 1996 and Kugakki kaeryang wiwŏnhoe 1998), at least 13 modified instruments have so far been exhibited. It is interesting to speculate whether North Korean modifications were familiar, but until the 1990s South Korean modifications did not alter the basic pentatonic tuning system. This does not imply that the North Korean modifications were not known about: North Korea exported some instruments to Japan (notably as a gift from the North Korean leader, Kim Il Sung, to a pro-North Korean arts troupe[17]), and from the late 1980s, North Korean texts and instruments were brought back to Seoul from Yanji. In the first modifications made in South

---

[16]   At a conference in Yanji of the People's Traditional Arts Study Association (Minjok Chŏnt'ong Yesul Haksulhoe) on 13 July 1999, Kim stated this work began in 1953, because only then had the war concluded; an audience member argued that 1952 was the appropriate date.

[17]   Some research on the zithers used by Koreans resident in Japan has been done by Inok Paek (2005). Following the end of the Pacific War, South Korea opened a brief repatriation programme for Koreans who had settled in Japan, the former colonial power, for work; North Korea did not do the same, hence the majority of Koreans who remained in Japan were

Korea, pegs replaced the cords, soundboard holes were added to increase volume, the material used for strings, bridges, resonators and pegs were changed, and in one case a device was even added to control the pitching of semitones (Chang Sahun 1993; Pak Pŏmhun 1991: 152–7). The *sanjo* maestro Sŏng Kŭmyŏn created and used a 15-stringed version in the 1960s that better facilitated modulation, adding strings between the first and second, third and fourth, and above the twelfth strings of the standard *sanjo* instrument; Sŏng's daughter recalls her mother had already used a 13-stringed instrument prior to the Korean War.[18]

A larger court *kayagŭm* offering greater volume was built by Yi Yŏngsu (b.1929) in 1982 for use in accompanying opera at the National Theatre. In 1985, the composer Yi Sŏngch'ŏn (1936–2003) commissioned a 21-stringed instrument from the maker Ko Hŭnggon that was first used in concert at the Munye Theatre in Seoul in October 1986. This added three additional bass strings and six higher-pitched strings, expanding the range to four octaves. The bass strings proved difficult to tune accurately, and so the instrument underwent subsequent modification, but once he had this new enlarged instrument, Yi used it in preference to traditional *kayagŭm* in his compositions. Ko told Howard in 1990:

> Twenty-one-stringed zithers are now typical of East Asia. The Korean version is not just an invention, because similar things exist elsewhere, but it was needed to allow the *kayagŭm* to cover a wider range. It can now produce as many sounds as Western instruments. It can reach lots of high pitches and all the low pitches. And it is larger, so it can create a louder sound. In other Asian countries, silk strings have been replaced, but this takes away the characteristic tone colour. We believe that the Korean colour should be retained, focussed in the centre of a tone.

The player Hwang Pyŏngju commissioned a 17-stringed instrument with polyester strings from the maker Pak Sŏnggi in 1986, combining in its tuning system both the court and *sanjo* instruments but eliminating the ram's horns and string coils. The tone is brighter and more resonant than traditional instruments (Hwang Pyŏngju 1990: 33–53) and this version became standard issue for the KBS Traditional Music Orchestra (KBS Kugak Kwanhyŏn Aktan) during the 1990s. In 1988, the player Pak Ilhun asked Ko to create an 18-stringed version that combined both traditional instruments but retained their materials and tone colour. The composer Pak Pŏmhun had a year before asked the same maker to create a trio of zithers; his mid-range instrument was similar to the *sanjo kayagŭm*, while a soprano version was narrower and shorter and a bass version larger. The Saeul Kayagŭm Trio achieved some fame using this set, playing pieces and arrangements by composers then working at Seoul's Chungang University.

---

for a number of decades considered sympathetic to North Korea. For information on their associations, see Sonia Ryang (1997 and 2000).

[18]   Thirteen-stringed instruments appear to have once been more common in North Korea, and, according to Pak Hyŏngsŏp (1994: 156), were frequently employed. Of potential interest, the related Mongolian zither, the *yatga*, was remodelled with thirteen strings in the 1930s. In Mongolia today, and across the border in Buryatia, scholars and performers state that this was remodelled on the basis of Korean instruments.

In 1989, Yi Sŏngch'ŏn returned to Ko to design a small children's instrument without the coils of strings. To this point, pentatonic tunings were retained.

Pak Pŏmhun next commissioned a 22-stringed instrument from Pak Sŏnggi, with a larger resonator and synthetic strings. This was first employed by Kim Il-ryun to premiere Pak's composition '*Sae sanjo*/New *Sanjo*' at the National Theatre in October 1995, but it proved difficult to use. Kim shortly afterwards approached another instrument maker, Cho Chŏngsam, who produced a 25-stringed instrument capable of heptatonic tuning and more able to be used for Pak's '*Sae sanjo*'. Ko subsequently produced his own version of this 25-stringed instrument.

And, no doubt, modifications will continue, not least due to a new fad: the *kayagŭm* ensemble. A decade after the Saeul Kayagŭm Trio, a quartet, Sagye, comprising four graduates of Seoul National University, held their premiere. Across Seoul, a *kayagŭm* orchestra was founded in Sookmyung Women's University led by Kim Il-ryun; other ensembles emerged, amongst them Yeoul, Gaya Beauty, IS (Infinity of Sound) and the family ensemble Lee Rang (comprising Mun Chaesuk and her two daughters). Ensembles call for new creativity from composers and arrangers, typically packaging the result as '*kugak* fusions'. They typically simplify ornamentation techniques, creating a harmonic, easy-listening repertory that is the scourge of many traditional musicians but is designed to appeal to new audiences for Korean music.[19]

---

[19] Selected recordings of the ensembles mentioned here are listed in the discography to this volume. Song Hyejin *et al.* (2005) provides a textbook-style account for devotees of the Sookmyung Kayagŭm Ensemble.

Chapter 3

My Musical Life and *Sanjo*:
Chaesuk Lee

Studying Korean Music

I was born on 31 May 1941. I started to learn Korean music in 1959, when I entered
university. I had planned to major in Western vocal music, because I had studied the
violin as a child and had learnt a little piano and singing, but during my third and final
year of high school at Seoul Women's Commercial High School I changed my mind and
decided I should take a degree in Korean music (*kugak*). That was exactly the same time
as Seoul National University opened the first course in Korean music, and I entered the
programme right at the beginning as one of the three students in the first cohort, majoring
in the 12-stringed long zither, the *kayagŭm*. I liked music very much, indeed it was my
primary interest, and one of my teachers told me I should enter the new programme,
because he thought that I would be able to be useful for my country in the future. In those
days, nobody knew much about Korean music, and I guess this explains why I started to
learn it rather late. I graduated with a BA in 1963, then entered graduate school as one of
only two students; I was the first to get an MA in Korean music.

Until the Seoul National degree course opened, Korean musicians concentrated
either on court music or folk music, and never played both repertories. Court music
experts couldn't play *sanjo*, our subject in this book and its accompanying recordings,
a genre for solo melodic instrument and drum accompaniment. Similarly, *sanjo*
musicians couldn't play court music. A *sanjo* musician played just one school of *sanjo*,
each school being based on one of the key master musicians of earlier generations,
and nobody played solo compositions for Korean instruments because, simply, there
weren't any pieces. In 1964, I gave the first solo recital on a Korean instrument in Korea,
on the *kayagŭm*, featuring all three styles of music – court, folk and contemporary
compositions. Before then, nobody had given such a recital. Why was mine the first of
its type in Korea? Well, one problem was that Koreans didn't want to hear a complete,
extended version of *sanjo* lasting about an hour; there was no audience.

At Seoul National, the new four-year curriculum was set up by Lee Hye-ku
(b.1909), the professor in charge, assisted by Chang Sahun (1916–1991). Chang
later became a professor. The curriculum required students majoring in performance
to learn all three styles of music – court, *sanjo* and new compositions. In the first
year, one learnt court music. In the second and third, one learnt primarily *sanjo*, but
in the final year, and in my case for just a semester, one was expected to master a few
contemporary compositions. Only then could one graduate. The repertory for court
music and folk music had a long history and was well settled, but new music needed
to be composed. As a *kayagŭm* major, I studied the literati ensemble *chul p'ungnyu*

Figure 3.1   Chaesuk Lee, photographed in 1994

and *sanjo* from Byungki Hwang (b.1936). Hwang's major had been law, but he worked as a lecturer at the Korean Music Department (*Kugakkwa*) from the opening of the programme. University lecturers were required to have degrees, but how could musicians qualify when nobody had graduated in Korean music? Hwang was asked to teach because he had learnt *sanjo* concurrently while doing his law studies. I learnt court music from Hong Wŏn'gi and Kim Yongyun, but I also learnt this same repertory from Hwang. Later, in 1973, I learnt more of the court vocal repertory for three months from Yi Ch'anggyu. When I started to teach after my graduation, I was expected to teach all three styles of court, folk and new compositions. In recent years, because my colleague Kim Chŏngja, who taught *kayagŭm* alongside me at Seoul National University, stopped playing *sanjo* and new compositions, so we divided the work between us: she taught court music while I taught *sanjo* and new compositions. In earlier years, though, we both played and taught all three styles.[1]

Learning and Notating the Schools of *Kayagŭm Sanjo*

When I was studying at college, there was virtually no notation for the repertory. In the case of *kayagŭm sanjo*, after Hwang had taught me by rote, I went home and wrote out the music to help me study what I was learning. The small amount of notation available used the old Korean mensural system known as *chŏngganbo*, but this only notated the basic musical elements, and so could only serve as a memory aid. Some people had experimented with writing court music and *sanjo* using this system, but I was the first to adopt staff notation for complete *sanjo* pieces. In 1971, I published the first complete *sanjo* notations, although Hwang had previously copied his own hand-written notation of a short version of Kim Yundŏk's *sanjo*. The important thing to repeat is that there was little notation when I began to study. Even when I had prepared my notation, I couldn't use it in a lesson since master musicians (*myŏngin*) considered it impolite. I learnt five *kayagŭm sanjo* schools from surviving masters between 1963 and 1969, beginning after I obtained my BA degree, which I notated in my 1971 book. None of the masters could read or write notation. It would not have been polite to record the lessons, so I had to learn by rote. The masters didn't like a student writing anything down during lessons, so I had to memorize the music. I would then go home and study what I had memorized, only at that point writing it down in staff notation.

For my MA dissertation, I wrote about rhythm in the *chajinmori* movement of *kayagŭm sanjo*. It is very difficult to match melody to *changgo* drum in the *chajinmori* movement, and my professor, Lee Hye-ku, asked me to explore why it was so difficult. He suggested I write a dissertation that would analyse the movement. So I did. I learnt three schools of *kayagŭm sanjo* and compared them, asking whether the movement was difficult in all *sanjo* pieces or just in some. This was how I first came to study different schools, working initially with the Kim Yundŏk, Kim Pyŏngho and Pak Sanggŭn schools. With the school of Kim Yundŏk, I had first learnt from beginning to end with Byungki Hwang during my BA course at Seoul National, but

---

[1]   Note that Lee retired from Seoul National University in 2005 and Kim in 2007.

then spent a further year learning directly from Kim. I was also able to work directly with Kim Pyŏngho and Sŏng Kŭmyŏn. At that time, I learnt just a 25-minute version of Sŏng's school. Actually, in my 1971 book, I called this the Pak Sanggŭn school because Sŏng herself called it Pak's school – she had learnt from Pak. Much the same happened with Kim Yundŏk, since his *sanjo* was really the school of Chŏng Namhŭi. In fact, saying it is Kim's school identifies a later player rather than the originator of the school; Pak Sanggŭn, in contrast, is the originator. The problem in the case of Kim was political: we were unable to call his *kayagŭm sanjo* that of Chŏng Namhŭi, because Chŏng had migrated to North Korea in 1947 and had settled there. In my MA dissertation, I actually wrote 'Chŏng OO', but in the 1971 book we thought it sensible to substitute Kim's name.

I first started studying with Kim Pyŏngho in 1963, when I was preparing my MA dissertation. I worked with him until he died in 1968. Initially, I only studied the *chajinmori* movement of his *kayagŭm sanjo*, but I returned to work with him in 1965, and learnt his complete piece before he died. I began working with Kim Chukp'a in December 1967, and I continued to work with her until she died in 1989. So, I learnt from her for more than 20 years. She, too, was from the same generation as Chŏng, Pak and Kim Pyŏngho, although for much of her life she had been a dutiful wife and had shied away from public performance. The master musician Kang T'aehong had passed away in the 1950s, before I began my study, although his was the fifth *kayagŭm sanjo* school I needed to learn. In 1967, I obtained a tape that he had recorded back in 1951 at a relative's house. But, although I had the tape, I didn't know exactly how to play his music – the fingering, the way of plucking strings, and the exact strings to be used to produce specific pitches were all problematic. I met his disciple, Kim Ch'unji, who couldn't play particularly well and who had forgotten many of the melodies, but when I reminded her, using my notation based on the old tape, she remembered each melody. She told me the appropriate fingering and plucking techniques. We worked together for almost a year. Within the state-funded preservation system, she was appointed 'holder' (*poyuja*) of Intangible Cultural Property 23, *kayagŭm sanjo*, in the early 1970s. Kang had three disciples, Wŏn Okhwa, Kim, and Ku Yŏnu. Wŏn, her elder, had died, and Ku was a little younger, so this was why Kim became the holder of the Property. Ku's widow, Shin Myŏngsuk, who had learnt a little from Kang when still a high-school student and who had then learnt from Ku, was nominated a holder of a provincial Property in Pusan, where she lived.[2] Kim herself died a long time ago, and there are no other successors to Kang's *kayagŭm sanjo* school.

In 1970, and over the next five years, I worked with Ham Tongjŏngwŏl, who was the disciple of Ch'oe Oksam and the inheritor of his *sanjo* school. I had by this time studied the six central *kayagŭm sanjo* schools, and I remain the only person who has learnt all six. Finally, in 1972, I worked with Kim Samt'ae on an additional school,

---

[2]   The state preservation system for arts and crafts was effectively founded with the passing of the Cultural Properties Preservation Law (*Munhwajae pŏp*) in 1962. By 2004, there were some 109 active national Intangible Cultural Properties (*Muhyŏng munhwajae*), about 40 per cent of which were performance arts. Alongside these, Properties are also appointed at provincial level; 288 were listed as active in 2004. For details, see Howard's *Preserving Korean Music* (2006).

that of Kim Chonggi. I have a transcription and have duplicated this, but I have never published it. I published my notation of Ch'oe Oksam's school (Lee 1980), and I've also published a book on how to play the hourglass drum *changgo* accompaniment to *sanjo*, having worked with the great drummer Kim Myŏnghwan, who was closely associated with the Ch'oe Oksam school as Ham's partner. As I had done with the *kayagŭm* parts, I wanted to learn from somebody from the older generation, hence I chose Kim Myŏnghwan. Although in the past accompanists adjusted what they played depending on the specific melodies offered by the soloist, by the time I worked on this book, they typically used stock drumming patterns. Many other scholars and performers have now followed my lead in preparing notations.

I performed the Kim Yundŏk *kayagŭm sanjo* in my first solo recital in 1964. In my second recital, in 1966, I gave the Sŏng Kŭmyŏn or Pak Sanggŭn *sanjo*. In my third recital, in 1975, I gave the Ch'oe Oksam *sanjo*, following this with the Kim Chukp'a school in my fourth recital in 1982.

In the 1970s, Sŏng migrated with her husband to Hawai'i, where she added a lot of melodies to her *sanjo* performance while keeping virtually the same structure. When she returned to Korea in 1984, I worked with her during her stay in a hotel for one month, studying with her every morning, and helping meet her costs. This allowed me to prepare my notation for her complete *sanjo*, which by then was about 65 minutes long, although she was no longer able to play the complete piece in one go. We used to play together and get through it. Sometimes, she would change the order of the melodies in a way that struck me as reflecting the notion that *sanjo* once had improvised elements. In reality, though, *sanjo* is today a tightly structured form revolving around a fixed sequence of movements, within which there are some flexible elements.

Byungki Hwang first learnt *sanjo* from Kim Yundŏk. Kim had learnt from Chŏng Namhŭi, but then added melodies of his own. He added half of the final movement, *tanmori*. When I later studied with Kim, I told him that I wanted to learn *sanjo* just as Chŏng had played it, and that was the piece that formed the basis of my 1971 notation. In the old days, *sanjo* masters taught just part of the final movement and told their students to compose their own way through to the end of the piece. In my 1971 volume, I, nonetheless, kept the *tanmori* movement just as Kim had taught it to me. When Kim was nominated as a holder of the Intangible Cultural Property for *kayagŭm sanjo*, he was criticized for playing a piece that was basically his teacher's piece. This was one reason why he added a lot of new melodic strands. He was very friendly with Kang T'aehong, and so he incorporated many of Kang's melodies. By developing his *sanjo*, he created his own school, demonstrating his appropriateness for appointment as a holder of the Property. His school is maintained by the current holder of the Property, Yi Yŏnghŭi. My 1971 notation, though, is based on what Chŏng taught Kim. In 1990, when Byungki Hwang visited North Korea as the leader of a performance troupe, he was able to get a tape of Chŏng playing his own *sanjo*, as he had developed it after leaving South Korea. A number of recordings of Chŏng from the 1930s also survive, and Hwang was able to use these materials to select and add melodies to what he had learnt from Kim Yundŏk, thereby recreating Chŏng's *sanjo* school. Hwang also added a few things of his own to bridge from one melodic idea to another, and he has now published both a notation and a recording of the resulting piece as a new *sanjo* school.[3]

As had happened with Kim Yundŏk, when Kim Chukp'a was nominated holder of the Property in 1978, she too added many melodies, enlarging her piece from 40 to 55 minutes in duration. She wanted to determine how *sanjo* would have been played in earlier times, and by the 1970s felt that a number of the schools sounded very similar. Kim, over the years and because she had been sequestered in marriage for so long, had forgotten some of what she had been taught, and after I had published my notation in 1971, she was able to start reconstructing parts that were missing. Then, because her piece developed, I published a new notation of its complete form (Lee 1983), just as I did with Sŏng Kŭmyŏn's enlarged, 65-minute *sanjo* (Lee 1987). I have also published a notation of Kang T'aehong's *sanjo* (Lee 1996). We should also mention another master musician, An Kiok. He also went to North Korea, like Chŏng Namhŭi, although while his style may have been different to that of Chŏng, the only comprehensive recordings we have date from after he left for the North, notably from his students in the Chinese Korean Autonomous Region of Yanji. I think, then, that by the time he made the recordings that survive, his *sanjo* had already changed a lot, and so it is difficult to say with any certainty which of his melodies predate the 1940s.

I was essentially Kim Chukp'a's first student. After she had been appointed holder of the Property for *kayagŭm sanjo*, she asked me to become her designated successor, her 'future holder' (*poyuja hubo*). The scholar Chang Sahun, though, advised me against agreeing, and I realized it would not be appropriate, since I had become a university professor. I taught a varied repertory, including new compositions and the different *sanjo* schools; I was not like the few who remained dedicated to maintaining a single *sanjo* school, like Ku's widow Shin Myŏngsuk, like Yi Yŏnghŭi, or like Sŏng Kŭmyŏn's eldest daughter, Chi Sŏngja (b.1945). Two performers who studied with Kim Chukp'a who are well known today are Yang Sŭnghŭi (b.1948) and Mun Chaesuk (b.1953). Both were students at Seoul National University, so from their second year they had to study *sanjo*; they both chose to work with Kim. Both, though, were trained within the university system, and after graduation established teaching careers in universities. Both were recently nominated as holders of the Property. To my mind, there is no need for two people of a similar age who specialize in the same *sanjo* school to be appointed. Besides this, *sanjo* is now popular, and teachers paid to work at universities don't need such appointments.

If we go back to the 1960s, people were appointed within the preservation system because they could not earn enough money to live on from practising their art or craft. There appeared to be no future for traditional arts without government sponsorship. Now, though, one can study Korean music performance at university, all the way through to a doctoral degree, and there are many who study *sanjo*. *Sanjo* performers with degrees can now work as professors in universities and the genre is no longer in danger of dying out. It is true that many other genres remain peripheral to the higher education system, like the literati instrumental ensemble music known as *Chul p'ungnyu* or *Hyangje chul p'ungnyu*, and these require support. But not *sanjo*. And professors, who teach and play court music, *sanjo*, and new compositions, can never be as sufficiently dedicated to a

---

3   Hwang Pyŏnggi (1998) and Sung Eum DE-0234 (1998).

single *sanjo* school as were the musicians of previous generations. Incidentally, I think it would be difficult for me to create my own *sanjo* school. Since I play all six of the existing major schools, I could theoretically choose elements from each to make my own version, but I do not consider I have anything to add to what is already present within the six core schools. There is no need for another school.

Drum Accompaniments, and the Effects of Notating *Sanjo*

When I began to learn *kayagŭm sanjo*, typical drum accompaniments for the first movement, set to the rhythmic cycle of *chinyangjo*, didn't always match the melodic content. *Chinyangjo* is a slow six-beat cycle that should be grouped in sets of four, or 24 beats. This is what I learnt from Kim Myŏnghwan, who was primarily a *p'ansori* accompanist but who also had a lifetime's experience working with *sanjo* musicians. Kim, of course, had no notation to work from, and so when he told me this it was before the idea became codified (notably in the writings of Paek Taeung, such as Paek 1979; 1981). But, if you look at my 1971 notations, lots of the sets appear to be incomplete, and a player will often move to a new melodic phrase halfway through the set. The reason Kim gave for maintaining sets of four *chinyangjo* cycles was that the set then matched the common *chungmori*, a 12-beat rhythmic cycle that is basic to Korean music. Simply put, a single six-beat cycle of *chinyangjo* has three articulated beats: a downbeat on the first beat, then drum sequences that fall on the fifth and sixth beats. Three beats are essentially silent, while all the accompaniment action comes on three beats. So, to give a complete set of 12 beats to match *chungmori*, you have to hear four *chinyangjo* cycles back to back. The same idea would apply to literati *kagok* lyric songs which, although most commonly set to a 16-beat cycle, have four empty beats, leaving 12 articulated beats. Again, variation form is used frequently in Korean music. So, in the literati instrumental ensemble suite that has become a staple for students, *Yŏngsan hoesang*, a 20-beat cycle is compressed in its variation to become a 10-beat cycle then a six-beat cycle (see Lee 1979: 10).

In *sanjo*, matching the accompaniment to the melody is difficult, because the drummer must be aware of exactly what is being played, rather than just play the model pattern of a rhythmic cycle. Many different melodies are played within the time-frame of a single cycle. If you look at *p'ansori*, the melodies tend to group in phrases that will be carried across a set of four rhythmic cycles, but in *sanjo* and other types of folk music the relationship is not so clear. There is a reason. If you think of the percussion bands of the Korean countryside known as *nongak* or *p'ungmul*, the instruments can never sustain interest over the 24 beats required across the four cycles of *chinyangjo*. The same applies to many folk singers. Not surprisingly, then, in much folk music *chinyangjo* is just six beats long, and nobody is concerned about joining four cycles together to form a larger set. It is more convenient to arrange a group of six beats, rather than continue a phrase over 24 beats. What, then, can we say? A theory exists, based on sets of four *chinyangjo* patterns and descending from the practice of *p'ansori* singers, but the reality can be different. So, if you look at Kim Chukp'a's *sanjo* as I notated it in 1971, the length of melodic strands was not always consistent, and some *chinyangjo* phrases lasted less than four cycles. In performance, an accompanist needs to recognize this and provide a cadence pattern for each strand, wherever the cadence comes. Later, Kim recognized the issue, and rearranged many of her melodic strands to fit the four-cycle scheme. Another famed accompanist, Kim Tongjun, incidentally, told me that the issue was more complex than always using sets of four cycles for *chinyangjo*, but he still taught the theory regardless of what he played. Practice, then, is at variance to theory.

Since I published my notation, my and other notations of *sanjo* have had considerable effect. There are two points about this that I want to mention. First, when I was studying at college, there was no notation, and so it was not possible to learn *sanjo* quickly. It took me some four years to learn a complete piece, and most of my near contemporaries during their university studies didn't get any further than a single movement of the piece, this being *chinyangjo*, the first and longest movement. So, without notation, it was not possible to maintain an adequate university teaching syllabus. Consider, too, the way that one learns within a university. You meet your teacher once a week or so, and there is insufficient time to imbibe the music through the age-old rote-learning system. From an educational point of view, then, having notations is absolutely necessary. Second, though, is the question of feeling and emotion. Most of this is difficult to notate, for most requires study by rote with a teacher. So, to develop the requisite feeling, I teach without notation. The notation becomes a memory aid that a student uses outside of the lesson, which allows them to learn to play the basic melodies. Once they have the basic melodies, we can work on emotion. At the same time, many *kayagŭm sanjo* schools are similar, so without notation few students would be able to accurately remember the subtle differences. Notation, then, is very helpful, and enables a student to efficiently learn the basic piece, but not to learn from beginning to end with no need for a teacher. Once a student has memorized the basic piece, I return to the rote method once more, and teach appropriate aesthetics, ornamentation and so on.

The Old and the New: Performing and Teaching *Sanjo* and New Compositions

In 1964 I gave my first public recital. I played '*Hahyŏn todŭri*', '*T'aryŏng*' and '*Kunak*' from the literati suite *Yŏngsan hoesang*. I played Kim Yundŏk's *sanjo*, accompanied on the *changgo* drum by Hong Kŏnja. And I played three compositions: Byungki Hwang's '*Sup*/Forest' (1963), a piece for *kayagŭm* – '*Kayagorŭl wihan sogok*/Small Piece for Zither' (1964) – written by the Seoul National University composer Chŏng Hoegap (b.1923), and Yi Sŏngch'ŏn's (1936–2003) '*Tokchugok 7-pŏn*/Solo No. 7' (1964). In my second recital, in 1966, I played Kim Yŏngjin's (b.1939) '*Sae sanjo*/ New Sanjo', Yi Sŏngch'ŏn's '*Norit'ŏ*/Playground' (1965),[4] Cho Chaesŏn's (b.1938) '*Shinawi*' and Paek Pyŏngdong's (b.1934) '*Shillaeak*' (with oboe, cello, drum and gong). Cho's piece was a concerto, and the orchestra was conducted by the scholar and musicologist Han Manyŏng. In 1967, I was awarded the Korean Music Prize (*Kugak sang*), and in 1974 I became the leader of the Seoul Metropolitan Traditional Music Orchestra (Seoul Shirip Kugak Kwanhyŏn Aktan), keeping this position for

---

4   First written for piano; Yi rescored 'Playground' for Lee's recital.

two years. I was the first female leader of the orchestra. Following my graduation, I was appointed an assistant in 1965, then part-time instructor at Seoul National University. I became a full-time lecturer when I was 26, in 1967, and later became the youngest professor. My classmates at Seoul National were Kwŏn Osŏng and Kim Yŏngjin; Kim Chŏngja, Song Pangsong, Lee Byong Won and Han Myŏnghŭi were in the second cohort who entered Seoul National in 1960. All of these have become important musicologists.

In 1964, I asked two composers to write pieces for my first recital. Yi Sŏngch'ŏn was studying in the Department of Korean Music; he had switched from studying medicine and had not yet graduated. There weren't any contemporary compositions that we could play except Byungki Hwang's 'Forest', and I wanted to play three new pieces. I asked Yi to compose for me, and because he was studying Korean music, he wrote a piece. He showed me what he had written and we discussed phrases that were difficult to play. In later years, our relationship worked in exactly the same way: he would discuss a composition with me and decide what needed to be changed to make the piece work on the *kayagŭm*. Similarly, Chŏng Hoegap wrote for my recital; he wrote his piece, showed it to me, and after discussion adjusted a few things. This became standard practice from the 1960s into the 1980s: composers would discuss their works with players and adjust them prior to a premiere. Players have a repertory of techniques specific to their instruments, and it is useful for them to work with composers to incorporate some of these, not least since at the time we had no equivalent of an orchestration book.[5] On the *kayagŭm*, for instance, players create the same pitch on two adjacent strings, using the left hand to sharpen the pitch of the lower-pitched string, and the effect is particularly characteristic. Or they play distinct ornaments, or use different fingers or distinct striking techniques. I never, though, have advised composers about their use of melody or structure, but have merely shown them how Korean styles, and particularly ornaments and fingering, can be incorporated. I have never forced composers to change their ideas.

Byungki Hwang is an exception amongst composers, because he is also an accomplished *kayagŭm* player. He doesn't need any advice on how to make his music idiomatic. Although he has often given the premiere of his own works, he has also written some pieces for other players. I've asked my colleagues at Seoul National University, such as Yi Sŏngch'ŏn and Paek Pyŏngdong, for pieces, and because they are friends who are interested in creating Korean-style music, they have generously created splendid works for me.

In my second recital, I performed Yi Sŏngch'ŏn's 'Playground'. This was Yi's breakthrough piece. It contained a lot of new techniques, such as arpeggios using both hands together above the bridges, that were very difficult.[6] The notation was so complex

---

[5]   Such as, for example, Walter Piston's *Orchestration* (1955/1969). The Korean situation has since changed, with, for example, books by Chŏn Inp'yŏng (1989) and Pak Pŏmhun (1991).

[6]   As discussed in Chapter 2, the strings of the *kayagŭm*, in both folk and court repertories, are plucked by the fingers of the right hand above the moveable bridges that define the sounding pitch while the fingers of the left hand add ornamentation or adjust the pitch below the bridges. The significance of the new compositions mentioned here is that, as with

that sometimes I could hardly read it. In one movement, '*Sonagi*/Shower', Yi used two similar bars of passagework to a section of the movement '*Pi*/Rain' in Hwang's 'Forest', although he changed the finger sequence. 'Playground' created a sensation, because it was so new, and many musicians, including my *sanjo* teachers, said I shouldn't play this kind of music. Sŏng Kŭmyŏn told me I was a bad person to even consider it. I was very concerned about the scathing criticism, but Lee Hye-Ku and Chang Sahun encouraged me, saying that we needed to create new music for the future.

A few years later, I played Yi Hyeshik's (b.1943) '*Hŭktam*/Mud Wall' (1969) in a concert for Liberation Day at the Citizen's Hall[7] and many people criticized me for playing such modernist music. I was very concerned until Han Manyŏng told me to read a specific book on modern European and American music.[8] I found the book in a shop, bought it, and still keep it. One chapter explains why people dislike new music when it is first performed, and suggests that unfamiliarity gives audiences difficulty. It cites the chaotic premiere of Stravinsky's 'Rite of Spring' and how, when Debussy's 'La Mer' was first performed in New York, a critic said it reflected a black and polluted sea, full of brass instruments sounding like frogs! Fifteen years later, when 'La Mer' was again performed by the same orchestra and conductor, the same critic wrote how beautiful it was. Ordinary people come to like new music over time. Through the 1960s, I premiered many of the new compositions written for the *kayagŭm*, and throughout my career I have been closely involved in creating a new history of *kayagŭm* compositions.[9]

New music developed very fast. We had known very few composers. Kim Kisu (1917–1986) was the first who wrote for Korean instruments. He primarily wrote orchestral and ensemble pieces, since his pieces were needed by the successor to court music institutes, the National Center for Korean Traditional Performing Arts, where he worked and where in the 1970s he became director. He wrote one or two pieces for his own instrument – the traditional transverse bamboo flute, *taegŭm* – but generally he based his style on traditional court and literati music, capturing the characteristics of Korean ornamentation in orchestral *tutti* that remained majestic and grand. Yi Sŏngch'ŏn and Kim Yŏngjin contrast Kim Kisu. Both graduated from Seoul National University with majors in composition, learning Western music as they studied, borrowing forms and structures from European art music, whereas Kim Kisu was a product of the court music institute. Other composers who write primarily for Western instruments have been more interested in expanding soundworlds, and have focused on the timbres of Korean instruments. Byungki Hwang, as an accomplished *kayagŭm* player, has tended to develop existing techniques for his personal instrument, coupling these to new ideas that sound good but also fit well under a player's fingers.

---

contemporary Japanese compositions for the *koto*, the fingers of both hands are used above the bridges to facilitate the playing of chords and complex passagework.

[7]   The forerunner to Sejong Cultural Center in downtown Seoul.

[8]   Howard and Lyons (1957). See the first chapter: 'What is modern music – and why have people never liked it at first?' (1957: 7–17).

[9]   Pieces premiered by Lee feature on an album, produced more as a historical document than as an album for listening (SRCD-9644; 2001).

When I gave my third recital, at the Arts Theatre in Myŏngdong in downtown Seoul in April 1975, Paek Pyŏngdong wrote '*Myŏng*/Inscription' (1975). I also played a piece by Yi Kangdŏk (b.1928), his 'First *Kayagŭm* Concerto' (1970), and gave the first Korean performance of Byungki Hwang's '*Ch'imhyangmu*/Dance to the Perfume of Aloes', a piece written in 1973 but premiered by the composer in Amsterdam in 1974. In 1972, Paek had written '*Shin Pyŏlgok*/New Piece', which Kim Chŏngja premiered, since she had asked him to compose the piece for her. I later played the piece for a concert of Paek's compositions. Later, I asked Paek to write another piece, '*Chŏngch'wi*/Atmosphere' (1977), for one of my students, and I helped that student work on it prior to the premiere; I played this same piece in my fourth recital in 1982. Some of Paek's pieces are complex and difficult, but they contain a concentration of techniques for the *kayagŭm*. This is particularly the case with 'New Piece', which makes it ideal alongside compositions by Yi Hyeshik and Yi Sŏngch'ŏn as a *kayagŭm* entrance exam piece at Seoul National. Actually, Yi Hyeshik's pieces are the most difficult to play.

Yi Sŏngch'ŏn's writing can also be difficult, but from 1986 onwards he concentrated on refining his writing for the new version of the *kayagŭm* with 21 strings that he had designed. Yi Sŏngch'ŏn tended to change the tuning for each piece he wrote and so, although initially the lowest strings were difficult to tune, he tended to raise their tuned pitches in later pieces to a degree that made them more easy to tune accurately. The advantage of Yi's 21-stringed instrument is that it produces Korean sounds, just like traditional instruments. This is not the case with the 22-stringed instrument introduced by the composer Pak Pŏmhun (b.1948) for his '*Sae Sanjo*/New *Sanjo*'. Kim Il-ryun premiered this piece in 1995, but it was so difficult to play that she commissioned the maker Cho Chŏngsam to add three more strings, thereby creating a 25-stringed *kayagŭm*. That, too, doesn't sound as Korean as Yi Sŏngch'ŏn's 21-stringed instrument.

To my mind, if new compositions are Korean, they should keep the pentatonic soundworld of traditional music. This happens on the 21-stringed *kayagŭm* because of its tuning, which is simply expanded at the bottom and top to give a four-octave pentatonic range. It is not the case on the 25-stringed *kayagŭm*, because the additional strings play pitches additional to the five pentatonic pitches. Also, many old techniques, such as using the fingers of the left hand beyond the moveable bridges to stretch or relax the string and thereby raise or lower the pitch, characterize the Korean soundworld, so an instrument should be able to facilitate them, just as the 21-stringed *kayagŭm* can. If a new zither is made that sounds like an orchestral harp, like a Japanese *koto* or a Chinese *zheng*, then to my mind it is no longer Korean.

What is a Korean soundworld? In 1988, the Korean Broadcasting System (KBS) asked the composer Yi Hyeshik to arrange Vivaldi's 'Four Seasons' for the *kayagŭm*. He did so, beginning with 'Autumn'. I was given the arrangement, designed to be played on one 21-stringed *kayagŭm* and three 12-stringed instruments. It was extremely difficult, and I felt that the sound was not good, because these zithers used silk strings and since, although tuned to a pentatonic scale, they were being required to play Western diatonic scales. However, I had a Chinese *zheng*, a superficially similar zither but with diatonic tuning and strings made from polyester and steel rather than silk,[10] and when I began to practise Yi's 'Autumn' arrangement on this it sounded good. So, although uncomfortable with saying so, I suggested we postpone the performance until we had a Korean *kayagŭm* with similar characteristics. In 1994, I set up the Korean Zither Musicians Association, and in 1998, when we held our first concert in Seoul, we finally premiered 'Autumn'. It now worked well, because we could use the new 25-stringed *kayagŭm*. The arrangement became something of a 'hit', because it suited youthful tastes, and one result was that four of my zither students created a quartet that was later named Sagye (Four Worlds).[11] A number of pieces have now been composed for Sagye, by Yi Sŏngch'ŏn and others, and a number of pieces arranged, from Vivaldi to compositions by the Argentinian *tango* maestro Astor Piazolla.[12] Recently, zither ensembles have become common. Our association is made up of university professors, and was set up partly to facilitate travel abroad to discover other Asian instruments and to increase the knowledge of Korean music amongst foreigners. However, since our first performance in Korea in 1998, we have invited performers of zithers similar to the *kayagŭm* – the Chinese *zheng*, Japanese *koto*, Vietnamese *dan tranh* and Mongolian *yatga* – to Seoul.

My Career: Past, Present, and Future

During my career, I have regularly given recitals. Beyond Korea, I have performed in Osaka and Tokyo (1967, 1987), Taipei and Kaohsiung (1976, 1983, 1990), Bangkok and Mahasarakham (1978, 1996), Cambridge, Durham, Edinburgh and London (1979, 1981, 2002, 2004), Hawai'i, Los Angeles, Washington, New York, Monteray, Berkeley, Chicago, Michigan, Detroit, San Diego, San Francisco and Colorado Springs (1979, 1985, 1987, 1996, 1998, 1999, 2000, 2006), Paris (1981), Bremen, Hanover and Köln (1981, 1983), Baghdad (1986), Hong Kong (1991), Beijing, Chengdu and Yanji (1994, 1995, 2001), Vancouver (1996, 2007), Podolsk in Russia (1997), and in Vietnam (2000, 2003). I have been visiting professor at the University of Cambridge (1979, 1981, 1983), at Hawai'i (1996) and at SOAS, University of London (2004). I have given workshops in Norway, Austria and the United States (1979, 1982, 1989). At Seoul National University, I have been Chair of the Korean Music Department (1980–1984, 1989–1991, 1995–1999), Head of the Asian Music Research Institute (1984–1988, 1994–1998) and Associate Dean (1991–1993). I have been a board member of the Society for Korean Music Educators since 1976 and of the Korean Musicological Society since 1991 (formerly, from 1975, I was

---

[10]   The modifications were made in the early twentieth century, as part of a Republic-era modernization drive that would later be inherited into socialist dogma (and thereby into North Korean policy) designed to both counter and embrace Western art music.

[11]   Four worlds of music: old, new, court and folk.

[12]   Sagye's first album, named simply with the group's name, was issued on the Polymedia label (n.d.), and was followed by a more cosmopolitan second, *Kayagŭm angsangbŭl Sagye 2 chip/Kayagum ensemble SAGYE part 2*, on EMI Korea (2004).

auditor). I have served on the advisory board of the National Center for Korean Traditional Performing Arts since 1995, and have been a board member for the Seoul City Cultural Property Committee since 1999.

In recent years, I have performed a complete *kayagŭm sanjo* virtually every year. In 1994, I gave the Kim Chukp'a *sanjo* school and in 1995, the Kang T'aehong school. In 1997, I gave the Sŏng Kŭmyŏn school and in 1998, the Kim Yundŏk school. In 1999, I gave the Kim Pyŏngho school and in 2000, the Ch'oe Oksam school. That was the year I was awarded the Great Korean Music Award by KBS. In 2002, I received the award of the National Academy of Arts, and in 2004 I was elected a member of the Academy. I retired at the end of August 2006, but have been made Professor Emeritus at Seoul National and Distinguished Professor at Hanyang University. I am republishing my notations of all six major *kayagŭm sanjo* schools, incorporating all melodies that the maestros introduced subsequent to my 1971 book, as I have documented them in later notations. These will be coupled to CDs of the *sanjo* masters playing their own pieces, taken from old recordings. I am also hoping to issue a double CD featuring my own 20-minute performances of each of the six *sanjo* schools I have worked on during my career.

Note

Based on interviews with Keith Howard at SOAS, University of London, 18 October and 25 October 2004. The reference list to this volume gives a list of Lee's primary publications; many compositions premiered by Lee were republished to celebrate her sixtieth birthday (in *Yi Chaesuk kyosu koegap kinyŏm haengsach'ujin wiwŏnhoe* (2001)).

Chapter 4

Analysis 1:
Mode, Rhythm and Regional Identity

Sanjo, putatively, emerged from folksongs, shaman music (particularly the instrumental improvisatory form known as *shinawi*) and *p'ansori*, epic storytelling through song.[1] All *sanjo* masters say this, although they rarely tie *sanjo* melodies to specific phrases in other instrumental or vocal genres. In the case of Kim Chukp'a's *kayagŭm sanjo*, the first movement does use one short motif very similar to a brief passage in '*Chŏksŏngga*/The Song of Chŏksŏng' from the repertory '*Ch'unhyangga*/ The Story of "Spring Fragrance"'.[2] In its *sanjo* incarnation, it is an important motif, returning in several movements. That the association should be so close is unusual amongst the various *sanjo* pieces of different schools. We note that many *sanjo* specialists learnt the self-accompanied song genre for the 12-stringed long zither, *kayagŭm pyŏngch'ang*, including Kim Chukp'a, Chŏng Namhŭi, Kim Pyŏngho, Sŏng Kŭmyŏn, Kang T'aehong and Ham Tongjŏngwŏl. Indeed, the close association is recognized at an official level, for *kayagŭm sanjo* shares a single designation with *kayagŭm pyŏngch'ang* within the South Korean preservation system as Intangible Cultural Property 23. *Kayagŭm pyŏngch'ang* comprise excerpts of *p'ansori*, short lyrical songs for warming up the voice known as *tan'ga*, and folksongs, but can hardly be considered evocative either of the extended solo vocalizations of *p'ansori* proper – in which a single performance can last several hours – or of the hour-long performance of a complete *sanjo*: few *sanjo* experts are also *p'ansori* experts.[3] The connection is with *kwŏnbŏn*, institutes for training entertainment girls that many *sanjo* specialists attended during the early twentieth century, where they learnt *kayagŭm pyŏngch'ang*, the literati song genres of *kagok* and *shijo*, and more.

Further, the standard transliteration of *sanjo* as 'scattered melodies' is misleading, since *sanjo* melodies are worked out in chunks, absorbing the general characteristics of the folk music of the south-western Chŏlla provinces as a regional accent, but few motivic specifics. Accent is coupled to local vocabulary in speech, allowing a Korean to tell where a person comes from. To give one example, until Kim Dae Jung assumed the South Korean presidency in 1998, officials in Seoul and abroad spoke either with a Seoul or a

---

[1]   Howard first coined this gloss for *p'ansori* in 1983. It is not easy to find a simple translation for the genre: 'solo opera' and 'musical storytelling' hardly do justice to the form. 'Epic storytelling through song' reflects the fact that the genre does have epic proportions, it is tradition making and tradition bearing, and it maintains and valorizes the performances of great teachers – as Chan E. Park (2003: 14–15) notes.

[2]   Often translated simply as 'The Story of Ch'unhyang', after the female heroine.

[3]   Chŏng Namhŭi was an exception: as well as recording *sanjo*, he starred as the hero in 1936 performances of a staged 'Story of "Spring Fragrance"' in Seoul, based on the *p'ansori* repertory.

south-eastern Kyŏngsang province accent, the latter area demarcated by the philosopher T'oegye in the sixteenth century as populated by the aristocracy. Kim, in contrast to earlier presidents, came from the south-western South Chŏlla province, so in 1998 officialdom began to bristle with the distinctive dialect of his home region. Similarly, it is said that a rural accent is key to success in North Korea, while a Seoul accent is an obstacle.

With *sanjo*, the dialect is a mix of mode, rhythm, and pitch treatment. Most *sanjo* players of the past hailed from the Chŏlla region. Many *sanjo* inflexions, then, may be present simply because the master who created the music came from Chŏlla. Kim Chukp'a, whose *kayagŭm sanjo* forms the basis of the analysis in this volume, was born in South Chŏlla province, and as she talked about *sanjo* she would often use dialect to express the correct attitude required of a performer for a specific musical phrase. For example, she described important melodic patterns as '*polsŏngŭm*', melodies that you should not let in one ear and out of the other. The primacy of Chŏlla was noted by the scholar Chang Sahun, who in the 1960s remarked in a class at Seoul National University how good it was that Chaesuk Lee, a native of Seoul, had learnt *sanjo* so well. This, he thought, promised a fruitful future in which regional barriers would be broken – if you like, the beginnings of a process of musical democratization that has indeed occurred as university training in traditional music has grown from its humble beginnings at Seoul National University in 1959. In reality, though, boundaries are there to be broken, and the migration of musicians during the twentieth century, notably to perform and live in Seoul, can be considered responsible for musical accretions in performance styles. Sŏng Kŭmyŏn, for instance, once sang a merchant's song to Lee, '*Mudŭrŏm saryŏ…*' used when selling radish and white cabbage, noting that this reflected Seoul dialect whereas *sanjo* was part of the south-western musical language. Yet, when she married a musician from the central Kyŏnggi province, Chi Yŏnghŭi, she added a little *kyŏngdŭrŭm* (also known as *kyŏngjo* – as marked in the score) to her playing, a style imitative of the lyrical and lively vocalizations of the central region. It is instructive to compare the *sanjo* playing of Sŏng's two daughters: while the elder, Chi Sŏngja (b.1945) preserves the sorrowful and plaintive *kyemyŏnjo* characteristic of Chŏlla, the younger, Chi Sunja, adds Kyŏnggi flavour.

Mode

Mode is one feature where knowledge of *p'ansori* aids the understanding of *sanjo*. Many Korean musicologists have written about mode, both in *p'ansori* and folksongs, including Yi Pohyŏng (1971 and many subsequent articles), Han Manyŏng (1972), Hahn Man-young (1974 and, for an English language summary, 1990: 161–89), Chang Sahun and Han Manyŏng (1975), Chang Sahun (1976), Paek Taeung (1982) and Um Hae-Kyung (1992).[4] In contrast, many writers on *p'ansori* as history or oral literature concentrate on styles of singing characteristic of individual masters and regions, including Chŏng Noshik (1940), Pak Hŏnbong (1966) Yu Kiryong (1980a–d) and Chŏng Pyŏnguk (1981). Essentially, three modes are carried across from *p'ansori* to *sanjo*, namely *kyemyŏnjo*, *ujo*, and *p'yŏngjo*,[5] although scholars

---

    [4]   For folksong modes and scholarly approaches to them, see Howard (1989: 147–50 and 2001: 191–4). For the discussion here on *p'ansori* modes we are indebted to Um Hae-Kyung (1992).

    [5]   '*Cho/-jo*' means mode, hence these would more accurately be rendered *kyemyŏn* mode, *p'yŏng* mode and *u* mode. For clarity, we have chosen to include the suffix.

do not agree on this. Yi Pohyŏng (1969) and Paek Taeung (1982), for example, consider the basic *sanjo* mode to be *kyemyŏnjo*; Kim Chŏngja (1969) and others distinguish between *kyemyŏnjo* and *ujo*; following a 1948 book by Ham Hwajin, Hwang Chunyŏn (1993), Yi Chiyŏng (1993) and Kwŏn Tohŭi (1993) consider the two core modes to be *kyemyŏnjo* and *p'yŏngjo*.

The first of the three modes, *kyemyŏnjo*, is routinely considered typical of south-western folksongs, notably *Yukchabaegi*, a characteristic song in a slow six-beat rhythmic cycle; Yi Pohyŏng (1969) notes that this mode is also used in shaman music from the Chŏlla region. Han Manyŏng identifies a 'tonal supply' of five pitches (1974: 311; 1990: 187–9) – g, a, c, d, e, where g is the dominant and c the tonic – giving a feeling roughly akin to a diatonic minor. *Kyemyŏnjo*, though, is more than a palette of pitches and, indeed, three characteristics apply: a central tone with very little vibrato (*ponch'ŏng*), a low 'vibrating tone' or 'trembling tone' (the *ttŏnŭn mok* or *ttŏnŭn ch'ŏng*) equivalent to the dominant, and a higher 'falling tone' or 'breaking tone' (the *kkŏngnŭn mok* or *kkŏngnŭn ch'ŏng*). Most scholars give primacy to the lower tone in the breaking-tone complex, and comment that the upper tone, as an appoggiatura, can be pitched from one semitone to a minor third higher (for example, Yi Pohyŏng 1971, Han Manyŏng 1973, Chang Sahun 1976). Paek Taeung (1982: 26–9) divides the breaking tone into its two components, a high acciaccatura (*kkŏngnŭn witch'ŏng*) and low resolving tone (*kkŏngnŭn araech'ŏng*). He notes a higher subdominant can also feature in modulation that he calls the 'irregular tone' (*ŏtch'ŏng*).[6] While the distinction between higher and lower tones is important in *p'ansori*, note that in *sanjo* a fast glissando is often used to join the two, utilizing a development of a characteristic ornament known as *chŏnsŏng* and necessitating that both are sounded on a single string with a single pluck. The combination of vibrating tone and breaking tone imparts emotional intensity, hence *kyemyŏnjo* is regarded as sad (*sŭlp'ŭn*), a sad mode (*sŏrŭmjo*) using a sad voice (*aewan ch'ŏng*).

Within *p'ansori*, though, *kyemyŏnjo* is not always cast with deep sadness, since it may have little vibrato or ornamentation. At such times, it often precedes modulation, and is considered to approach a second mode, *p'yŏngjo*. A further differentiation is made where the upper and lower parts of the breaking tone are given as separate and distinct tones, hence Paek Taeung (1982: 30–31; cited in Um 1992: 137–42) reports that singers talk about three versions of the mode, namely the highly ornamented *chin kyemyŏnjo*, *p'yŏng kyemyŏnjo* with less vibrato and ornamentation, and an in-between version that separates out the breaking-tone constituents, *tan kyemyŏnjo*. The notion of an in-between version links to a particular *p'ansori* style known as the Kangsan school, believed to have been initiated by Pak Yujŏn, a nineteenth-century singer famed at the court specifically for softening the folksy nature of *kyemyŏnjo* to appeal to his urban audience (Park 2003: 180), but also associated with a melodic type developed by the central Kyŏnggi Province singer, Mo Hŭnggap.

Some writers on *p'ansori*, following Chŏng Noshik's (1940) collection of singers' biographies, have for many years tended to consider the Kangsan style almost synonymous to the so-called Western school, *Sŏp'yŏnje* (for example Pak Hŏnbong 1966; Kang Hanyŏng 1977; Chŏng Pyŏnguk 1981). The Western school is lyrical,

---

6   One might consider the theoretical basis for this to equate with the octotonic (or eight-tone heptatonic) scale discussed in some Chinese music scholarship; the eleventh harmonic, which would be tuned somewhat sharper than the subdominant, is commonly utilized for modulation.

emotional and perhaps slightly feminine, the emotion imparted by a strong *kyemyŏnjo* presence. Contrasting the Western school is the more masculine and majestic Eastern school, *Tongp'yŏnje*. To Chŏng Noshik (1940: 10–11), the Eastern school developed to the east of the Sŏmjin River (Kangsan, incidentally, is situated where this river meets the mountains), taking on a specific singing technique associated with the great singer Song Hŭngnok.[7] In contrast, the Western school, *Sŏp'yŏnje*, in recent times revived overnight in 1993 with the film of the same name directed by Im Kwŏnt'aek,[8] was based on the singing style of Pak Yujŏn and developed in Kwangju, Naju and Posŏng. The styles are not as clear-cut as we might wish, as Um (1992: 185–6) has shown: Chŏng (1940: 10), for instance, describes the Western school metaphorically as rich, like meat, or like a garden filled with ten thousand flowers, and the Eastern school as plain, like vegetable dishes, or like a moon rising from thousands of mountains; Yu Kiryong (1980c: 20–21) gives the former as soft, sentimental, sorrowful, like the speech of a gentle person, and the latter as virile and spirited yet dignified, like the speech of somebody gallant; Pak Hŏnbong (1966: 67) contrasts the two as spring/male (Eastern school) and autumn/ female (Western school). Again, the celebrated drum accompanist Kim Myŏnghwan (1913–1989) described the Western school as fishing with a net of tightly knit mesh and the Eastern school as fishing with a net of big mesh (in Chŏng Pyŏnguk 1981: 55–6); to Lee, he further commented that the Eastern school used less vibrato than the Western school because it developed amongst the high mountains of Korea's spine.[9]

While the Western school emphasizes *kyemyŏnjo*, the Eastern school features more *ujo* and the Kangsan school more *p'yŏngjo*, and this becomes a criterion for distinction.[10] None of these modes, though, is used to the exclusion of the others (as Chŏng Pyŏnguk notes; 1981: 52), so it might be better to follow Chan E. Park and introduce a geomantic notion: '[d]eveloped on the slopes of spectacular Chiri Mountain, the Eastern school manifests the strength and stately bravery of *ujo*; bred on the plains of Chŏlla along the coastal horizons, the Western school features the doleful *kyemyŏnjo* with nostalgically drawn-out sentence endings' (Park 2003: 179).

Ujo and *p'yŏngjo* have counterparts in court music, and Yi Pohyŏng (1982: 250) writes that *ujo* remains similar to the mode used in the classical vocal genres of *kagok* (lyric songs) and *shijo* (sung poems). *Ujo* is grand and magnanimous, in musicological accounts characterized as using the pentatonic scale a, c, d, e, g. In *p'ansori* it is associated with solemnity, seriousness or the actions of the aristocracy and court officials. The associations are rendered through almost declamatory sections in melodic sequences featuring melodic leaps of up to a fifth or sixth. Melismas join these intervals and, in contrast to *kyemyŏnjo*, the pitch at the end of phrases tends to

---

[7]   Born around 1790.

[8]   *Sŏp'yŏnje*, based on the novel by Yi Chŏngjun with music by Kim Soochul, tells the story of a poverty-stricken father's attempts to train his daughter to become a singer; to engender her correct attitude to suffering, he deliberately blinds her. Heather Willoughby has provided musicological considerations of the film and its relation to *p'ansori* (Willoughby 2000, 2003).

[9]   Kim may well have been making oblique reference to the sixteenth-century characterization of Korean regions by T'oegye, who referred to the people of Kyŏngsang province to the east as aristocrats looking down on others from lofty peaks.

[10]   In relation to, for example, nominations within the Intangible Cultural Properties system (see Park 2003: 179; Howard 2006 [*Preserving Korean Music*]: Chapter 3).

rise or remain constant, rather than falling away. *Ujo* makes limited use of vibrato or glissando. *P'yŏngjo* is less grand, as is fitting for a term where the first syllable (as a Sino-Korean character) can signify the everyday and ordinary. It uses pentatonic materials: g, a, c, d, f. Within it, the f can fall to, or be pitched closer to, e. In *sanjo*, its use is associated with a defunct *p'ansori* style, the so-called Central school (*Chunggoje*), once centred on an area bordering Ch'ungch'ŏng province to the north and north-east of Chŏlla, associated with singers who flourished in the nineteenth century such as Yŏm Kyedal – a native of the region – Kim Sŏngok and Mo Hŭnggap (Chŏng 1940; Pak Hŏnbong 1966; Yu Kiryong 1980a–g) and, arguably, the recently departed Pak Tongjin (1917–2003; Yi Kukcha 1988: 204).

In terms of *kayagŭm sanjo*, modal considerations largely stem from *kyemyŏnjo*, used with the full gamut of vibrating tone, steady tonic and breaking tone, and present with its constituent tonal palette. Where the characteristic tonal treatment is lacking, then the Kangsan school is typically evoked, moving towards *p'yŏngjo* and *ujo*. Sometimes, the tonal palettes of these latter modes displace that of *kyemyŏnjo*, becoming the key organizing feature for a melodic block. Sometimes, though, *p'yŏngjo* or *ujo* are merely hinted at. Their distinction, then, is a matter of degree. Performance intent is what matters, and it is vital to bear in mind that Kim Chukp'a described specific melodic sections of her *sanjo* as being in *kyemyŏnjo*, *p'yŏngjo* and *ujo* modes, but also some sections as being representative of the Kangsan school. She could do so, at least in part, because of how the modes are represented – as sets of specific pitches – on the zither itself. For *sanjo*, the *kayagŭm* is tuned to a pentatonic scale, the 12 strings giving a range of two and a half octaves: G–c–d–g–a–c′–d′–e′–g′–a′–c″–d″. Within this, *kyemyŏnjo* is usually given with c as the central tone (g–a–c–d–e), g as the vibrating tone and e falling to d as the 'falling tone'. *Kyemyŏnjo* may modulate up a fifth (to d as vibrating tone, g as central tone, and c falling to a as the 'falling tone'), without causing any major tuning difficulties but at the same time illustrating that the interval between the two components of the 'falling tone' need not always be a major second. On the instrument, *ujo* comprises a–c–d–e–g, and is typically perceived by performers as a shift of pitch up one tone from the regular *kyemyŏnjo*, while *p'yŏngjo* comprises g–a–c–d–f, the f marking it as distinct but falling to e when the Kangsan school is invoked. Since no string is pitched to f, this tone is produced by raising the pitch of the e string by pushing down to stretch it beyond the bridge – hence the tendency to fall back to e.

Analysis

The recording by Chaesuk Lee of Kim Chukp'a's *kayagŭm sanjo* included with this volume is based on Kim's performance shortly before her death. Lee first published a notation of this in 1971, based on Kim's piece before she expanded it following her appointment as holder of the *sanjo* Intangible Cultural Property. Her second notation, completed in 1982 and published first in 1983 (but then republished in 1986 and 1988), was based on a specific recording made by Kim accompanied on *changgo* hourglass drum by Kim Tongjun, and this second version is used as the basis for the score given in this volume on page 91.

Tasŭrŭm

Performers consider that the opening section of *sanjo*, formerly an improvised tuning section, should set the scene with elegance. Hence, the most appropriate mode is *ujo*, the melodic path incorporating large intervallic jumps, and the melodic style at times approaching declamation. The feeling of elegance is enhanced by a lack of metre, and performers claim not to consciously maintain any specific pulse. Players introduce the gamut of techniques available to them within *tasŭrŭm*: vibrato, acciaccature and portamenti, plucking techniques and ornaments. The left-hand ornaments include *chŏnsŏng*, where the string is pressed sharply and quickly released (note that in *kyemyŏnjo* the breaking tone is captured by striking the string after it has been pressed and then releasing), *t'oesŏng*, where the string is pulled to lower the pitch, and *ch'usŏng*, a slow rise in pitch created by gradually pressing the string.

Tasŭrŭm comprises a sequence of phrases, marked by double vertical slashes; each phrase is perceived as an entity. It divides into two halves, each ending with something akin to a full cadence (phrases 5 and 14). The last of these creates closure as the accompanist joins. A related passage ends the second phrase, almost before the music has got going. In the first half, the use of the tone a at the end of phrases creates a half close, given space with a fermata (phrases 1, 3, 4, 6). In the second half, the fall in pitch across a second from d to c creates something of a sob – the descending ending common in *kyemyŏnjo* phrases – but on each occasion recovers, leading us on to the next melodic strand (phrases 8, 9, 10, 11, 12, 13). A sense of modulation comes as phrase 7 segues to phrase 8, the former ending on d (the tonic in *ujo*) and the latter on c (the tonic in *kyemyŏnjo*). The pitch a is given considerable emphasis, the dominant within *ujo* but, following Paek Taeung's observation, the submediant of *kyemyŏnjo*. Overall, though, *tasŭrŭm* offers little sorrow, for no single tone is given any significant vibrato, and there is no breaking tone. Hence, although *kyemyŏnjo* lurks beneath the surface, *ujo* remains the primary mode. In the first three phrases, the pitch a is approached in a number of ways: as the resolution to acciaccature played on the neighbouring string at the same pitch, rising from a fourth below or falling from a third above; as a sustained tone given a sound envelope that lowers then restores the pitch; approached through a sequence of pitches imitative of typical *p'yŏngjo* patterns falling across a fifth; with slight vibrato.

Each movement after *tasŭrŭm* is allied to a single rhythmic cycle, a *changdan* (lit.: 'long short'). Each rhythmic cycle is metrical, with a distinct downbeat and internal points of accent: these features prescribe a code. The code establishes a model, the length of which is rigidly maintained, that each musician uses as the basis for extemporization. Model patterns, as widely taught to students of Korean music, are given in Notation 4.1. The drum that today is virtually ubiquitous to Korean music is the double-headed hourglass drum, *changgo*. This is a flexible instrument that for the accompaniment of *sanjo* is played by the hand and a thin whip-like stick (the *yŏl ch'ae*). The hand produces a thud on the lower-pitched drumhead, while the stick is used on the higher-pitched drumhead to create acciaccature, rolls, single strikes and multiple strikes. In the score below, the convention we adopt is to notate hand strikes below a single line with tails going down and stick strikes above the line with tails up.[11]

---

[11]   Howard (1998) explores the use of notation for Korean music, explaining how and why this modified form of staff notation has come to be commonly used by Korean and foreign musicologists alike. See also Lee Byong Won 2000.

Chinyangjo

Chungmori

Chungjungmori

Chajinmori

Hwimori

Sesanjoshi

Notation 4.1 Rhythmic cycles (*changdan*) used in Kim Chukp'a's *sanjo*

Chinyangjo

Chinyangjo is the first movement proper of any *sanjo* piece. A number of Korean musicians have in recent publications dropped the last syllable, *-jo*, calling this movement '*chinyang*'. This, according to Lee Hye-ku,[12] is incorrect, because the name comes from Chŏlla, where it was formerly referred to as *chinjo*, '*chin*' meaning long or slow (a dialect form of '*kin*')[13] and '*-jo*' in this case meaning piece. It may be of significance that the *chinyangjo* movement in *sanjo* appears to have been influenced by the melodic improvisations of shaman rituals, *shinawi*, where it typically marks an interlude, or the preparation of either the altar or ritual paraphernalia.[14] It is possible to suggest that the term '*chinjo*' or '*chinyangjo*' was added after the movements of *sanjo* had been created as a sequence within a piece, indicating that this movement, in comparison to the others, is both long and slow.

The melodic phrasing of the *chinyangjo* movement in *sanjo* is distinct from that favoured within *p'ansori*. However, to the great accompanist Kim Myŏnghwan, where *chinyangjo* appears in *p'ansori* it marks sets of four six-beat cycles in compound metre (18/8). To reflect this, some scores give the metre as 24 x 3/8. *P'ansori* texts often continue across all four cycles, creating extended phrases (the pace is so slow, however, that singers do not sing the entire phrase in one breath). The four cycles have distinct roles and characteristics in the sequence, typically being described as *ki*, *kyŏng*, *kyŏl* and *hae*, or, in English, 'rise, hang, bind, loosen' (Yi Pohyŏng 1973: 217). The first in the sequence establishes tension, its fifth and sixth beats stretching upwards in anticipation; the second ends with a half-cadence, a mid-point approaching relaxation; the third develops tension; the fourth resolves and cadences. The downbeat of each cycle is distinct, but must distinguish between the beginning of *ki* and the other three cycles in the set. Thus, when teaching students *chinyangjo* accompaniment patterns, Kim Tŭksu (1917–1990) used to teach that the *ki* downbeat should be played as a simultaneous strike on both drumheads, the downbeat of *kyŏng* and *hae* should be played by the hand on one drumhead alone, and that of *kyŏl* should be softest of all.[15] The accompanists Kim Myŏnghwan and Kim Tongjun (1928–1990), in contrast, gave *kyŏl* in a similar way to *kyŏng* and *hae*.[16]

Note that it is the melodic instrument that sets the pace, hence the initial downbeat of *chinyangjo* may not be sounded by the drum. Each of the four cycles is taught to incorporate specific percussion patterns for beats five and six. Kim Myŏnghwan would offer dotted crotchets for *ki*, more activity in *kyŏng* and *hae* (dividing the two beats into quaver+crotchet and crotchet+quaver, with additional acciaccature) and, typically, a single strike on beat five for *kyŏl* followed by silence on beat six. He added cosmological significance to this, dividing the four cycles into two pairs, the former *ŭm* (Ch: *yin*) and the latter *yang*, then subdividing each pair into an initial *ŭm* and a subsequent *yang*, and

---

[12] Personal communication to Chaesuk Lee.

[13] The verb is *childa/kilda*.

[14] An example would be in Chindo *Ssikkim kut* – listen to the first track on *Shamanistic Ceremonies of Chindo* (JVC VICG-5214, 1993).

[15] Howard took lessons from Kim in 1983.

[16] All three accompanists were, during the latter years of their lives, holders of the Intangible Cultural Property for drum accompaniment (formerly Property 59; now part of Property 5).

finally dividing each six-beat cycle into an initial four-beat *ŭm* – the emotional core, to Ham Tongjŏngwŏl the *chŏnbanbu* or 'fore part' – and a second articulative *yang* on beats five and six – the *hubanbu* or 'after part' to Ham. This distinction embodies energy (Kor: *chi*; Ch: *qi*) as the interplay of two opposites: *ŭm* dark, black, negative, the receptive female and below; *yang* light, red, positive, the penetrating male above.

Lee Hye-ku and Chang Sahun have identified a reductive principle that can be applied to Korean music analysed over chronological time (that is, through a comparison of historical scores, arranged from oldest to youngest) (see, for example, Lee 1981a, 1981b, 1981c). One feature is that melodic variants speed up as the metrical length reduces. Lyric songs, *kagok*, reduce from 16 beats to 11 per cycle, while in the literati suite *Yŏngsan hoesang* successive movements reduce from 20 beats to ten then to six. By the same logic, a five-beat metre reduces to three then two. The principle involves cutting and omitting silent beats (that is, where the model rhythmic cycle features rests or silence). *Chinyangjo* can be subjected to the same reductive principle: three beats of each cycle provide the articulation (beats one, five and six), while three feature melodic elaboration but no drum accompaniment in the model cycle (beats two, three and four). If these three silent beats are cut, each cycle is reduced to a three-beat core. Four cycles set end-to-end in sequence then give four sets of three – that is, twelve in total. The significance of this resides in the structure of subsequent *sanjo* movements (and other Korean music), since compound quadruple metres (12/8 or 12/4) are common. Indeed, the second movement of all *sanjo* pieces, *chungmori*, uses a 12/4 rhythmic cycle where the model pattern consists of four sets of three beats. Hence, sets of four *chinyangjo* cycles create balance and unity.

Juxtaposing this observation with cosmological ideas inherent in the Taoist-inspired *ŭm/yang* philosophy allows us to suggest that the set of twelve – four *chinyangjo* cycles, or one *chungmori* cycle – is a microcosm of *sanjo*. Within the set, a sequence of tension and relaxation (or resolution) applies. The *sanjo* master Shim Sanggon once remarked to Lee Hye-ku that this was exactly how *sanjo* worked: '*Choeŏtta p'urŏtta hanŭn kŏsijiyo*' ('It is a thing of tightening and loosening'); Lee, in a more scholarly way, referred to the sequence as '*Kinjanggwa iwan*' ('tension and slackness'). At the macro level, *sanjo* moves from the highly emotional *chinyangjo* to a resolution in an extremely fast 4/4. Each movement, similarly, moves from tension to relaxation. And, within the schema set out above, each set of four *chinyangjo* cycles (or each *chungmori* cycle) does the same.

Without song texts providing grammatical constructions to mark the extended phrases it is, however, impractical for a *sanjo* player to count the 24 beats required if *chinyangjo* is rendered as a set of four six-beat cycles. Rather, there is a tendency to reduce phrase lengths. This is not unlike common folksong practice,[17] but has the effect of undermining the sequence of four cycles. Despite this, a drum accompanist must vary both the initial downbeat intensity and the treatment of each fifth and sixth beat to match melodic phrasing. In doing so, some of the distinctions made in the four-cycle sequence are maintained. This is clear in Lee's 1983 transcriptions, where she includes the accompaniment of Kim Tongjun, one reason being so her students

---

[17] As shown with respect to the south-western folksong *Yukchabaegi* by Howard (2004: 161–4).

could practise the drum accompaniment.[18] This takes us back to the early 1970s, when Seoul National University moved its campus to the foothills of mountains on the southern periphery of the capital from its former central Seoul location.[19] Accompanists had been readily available in town, but it was now expensive to bring them to the new campus for just a few hours a week, and so Lee taught using her own drum transcriptions.

In the recording Lee used as the basis of her 1983 transcription, Kim Tongjun tried to match Kim Chukp'a's playing. He anticipated what would come next, giving appropriate cadential patterns and often falling into the four-cycle sequence, but the result demonstrates that the ideal is far from the reality. Looking at the melodic treatment, marking *ki, kyŏng, kyŏl, hae* as 1, 2, 3 and 4 respectively, and using square brackets to indicate melodic strands and sub-strands, Kim Chukp'a gave the following sequence of cycles: [1a] 1, 2, 3, 4 / [1b] 2, 2, 4 / [1c] 1, 2, 2, 2, 2, 2, 2, 4 / [2a] 1, 3, 2, 2, 4 / [2b] 1, 2 / [3a] 2, 2, 2, 3, 2, 4 / [3b] 2, 2, 3, 4 / [4] 2, 2, 2, 4 / [5] 1, 2, 3, 4, and so on. Clearly, 2, the half-cadence *kyŏng*, was most frequent. Because *kyŏng* can mark the end of a phrase, many phrases lasted just the six beats of a single *chinyangjo* cycle. Note, too, that Kim Chukp'a joined single-cycle phrases together, as she divided her piece into a sequence of what she termed *karak* ('melodies'), based on mode and modal shift. Each 'melody' could contain multiple phrases, hence, given the complexity involved, an alternative way of considering 'melodies' is as 'paths'.[20]

The first four cycles of Kim Chukp'a's *chinyangjo* movement and their melodic treatment appear to fit the four-cycle sequence closely, but on closer inspection the melody at the end of the third cycle, with an acciaccatura e preceding an a held for two beats, is cadential. It is only with hindsight that listeners realize this was not meant to give any relaxation, since the melody moves on into the fourth cycle, the e returning on the downbeat and rising to a after a crotchet. Things began to go awry in cycle five, where Kim Chukp'a gave an ending indicative of *kyŏng* (2), but the drummer offered a *ki* (1) pattern; as Kim Chukp'a presented a further *kyŏng* in cycle six, the drummer stuck with *ki*; both gave *hae* (4) in cycle seven, rather than cycle eight. Both musicians agreed to end cycle eight as *ki* (1), but there was a hiccup in cycle 10, where the accompanist anticipated the zither melody by incorrectly initiating *kyŏl* (3) only to recover on the sixth and final beat to correctly play *kyŏng* (2). Cycles 11–14 were all given as *kyŏng* (2) by Kim Chukp'a, but if the drummer had matched her he would have risked sounding repetitious, so he offered the sequence *ki, kyŏng, kyŏng, ki* – the last sounding slightly awkward since the zither's appeal to relaxation (created because her *kyŏng* ended with a half-cadence) was met by the drummer increasing tension (the 'rise' of *ki*). The performers agreed

---

[18]   Space prevents us giving the drum accompaniment of Kim Tongjun here, but all of Kim Chukp'a's melodic phrases are retained by Chaesuk Lee in both the notation and recording.

[19]   In central Seoul, the Department of Traditional Music had been housed in Hyehwa-dong and then Ulchiro 6-ga.

[20]   Kim Haesuk, in her book on *sanjo*, uses the term *karak* in a slightly different way, distinguishing between 'stereotyped' and 'scattered' types (1987: 81). In the SamulNori percussion quartet and amongst some earlier drummers such as Kim Pyŏngsŏp (1921–1987), '*karak*' defines variants of model patterns. '*Karak*' can also mean component parts, as in *son karak* (fingers).

on a resolution in cycle 15, with *hae* (4). Again, the melodic phrasing on beats five and six of cycle 18 suggest we have reached a further *hae*, and this was what the drummer assumed, only to discover that the zither player intended to continue across the bar line; with hindsight, the drummer should have played a *kyŏng* pattern. In the third 'melody' (cycle 23 onwards), the mix of agreement and uncertainty continued: cycles 23 and 25 both feature a zither *kyŏng* (2) that contrasts the drum *ki* (1), but the *hae* (4) cadences in cycles 28 and 32 match perfectly.

To what extent was the uncertainty real or imagined? Most likely, the reason why Kim Tongjun had a tendency to relate to the four-cycle sequence was because he was primarily a *p'ansori* accompanist, just as were Kim Myŏnghwan and Kim Tŭksu. Indeed, Kim Tongjun was also an accomplished *p'ansori* singer.[21] Equally important may be the fact that Kim Chukp'a was not a *p'ansori* singer, so had less experience of conceiving of phrases spread across sets of four *chinyangjo* cycles.

Kim Chukp'a divided her *chinyangjo* movement into 12 'melodies';[22] these are marked in the score using square brackets. The first is in *ujo* mode, continuing from the introduction. It brings the first reference to *p'ansori*, and to the specific 'Song of Chŏksŏng', in a falling a–e–d motif. The highest of these pitches, a, is typically given a falling and rising portamento, a–g–a, obtained by the left hand pulling then loosening the string beyond its bridge; e is often sharpened, almost to an f, achieved by plucking the e string while raising the pitch by tightening (pushing) the string beyond the bridge. The first intimation of the a–e–d motif comes on the second beat of cycle 1; it is given more fully on the second and third beats of cycles 2 and 4, with an echo on the third beat of cycle 3. An octave lower, the pattern reappears on beats two and three in cycles 7 and 9, the latter teasing out pitch ambiguity between f and e, just as happens transposed down a fourth in cycle 6 (e/d/e–c–b–a, and so on). The motif subsequently recurs, in cycles 11, 12, 13, 15, 30, 31, 32, 37, 38 and 42, usually on the second and third beats. The transposed treatment in cycle 6 gives rise to a number of additional melodic extensions, but this motif functions as a primary melodic device for the first six 'melodies'.

On the fourth beat of cycle 4, *ujo* mode is threatened by a pattern that combines an initial ascent with a fall to outline a virtual triad; this signals a change in central tone to c. In effect, cycles 1 to 4 constitute a microcosm of the whole movement: all *chinyangjo* movements end in *kyemyŏnjo* mode, and here the first *p'ansori*-influenced sequence of four cycles ends with a glimpse of *kyemyŏnjo*. An additional point to note is that a relatively narrow range is used throughout the opening 'melody', running from cycle 1 to cycle 15,[23] coupled to an infrequent use of vibrato that enforces a feeling of restricted emotion appropriate to *ujo* mode.

The second 'melody', cycles 16–22, introduces the vibrating tone as a low dominant, a, contrasting it with the steady central tone, d. While the pitch envelope used for vibrato increases, the material remains unconvincing as *kyemyŏnjo* mode, but does not need to be otherwise: Ham Tongjŏngwŏl provided the key to understanding when

---

[21] His rendition of '*Chŏkpyŏkka*/Song of the Battle at the Red Cliff', with accompaniment by Han Ilsŏp, was re-released on CD in 1998 by Synnara (NSSRCD-003).

[22] Here, for clarity, we retain quotation marks around these large sections, Kim's '*karak*'.

[23] We are reminded of Debussy's 'Syrinx' and Varese's 'Density 21.5'.

she referred to 'adding colour' (*saekkal naenda*), the colour of *kyemyŏnjo*, without modulating to it. So, we may state that Kim Chukp'a gives *kyemyŏnjo* colour while retaining *ujo* mode. Chaesuk Lee, reflecting Kim's personal designation, calls this '*kyemyŏnsŏng*'. The third 'melody', cycles 23–32, adds the next element of *kyemyŏnjo* proper, the breaking tone. Beginning with an unstable g in cycle 23, the breaking tone is expanded into a g–f portamento on beat 5 in cycle 23, beat 2 in cycle 24 and beat 2 in cycle 25. Cycle 28 shifts the central tone back to d, preparing for this in cycle 27 as the tone a is repeated with vibrato, thereby emphasizing its role as a dominant. The central tone is emphasized in beats 5–6 of cycles 31 and 32, and then a bridge section (*tol ch'ang*) – the fourth 'melody' – is initiated that gradually drops the central tone one tone, to c. Beat 2 in cycle 33 indicates the shift about to happen, but the last two beats of cycles 34 and 35 continue to play on ambiguity before cycle 36 firmly resolves onto c.

With c established as the new central tone, the fifth 'melody' (cycles 37–44) can start afresh. We have, though, moved away from *kyemyŏnjo*, but now to *p'yŏngjo*. One tone marks this mode out and creates distinction: f (fa, the subdominant). Put simply, this pitch is not part of the *kyemyŏnjo* palette. It is initially approached in an echo of the falling motif, the f tempted downwards towards e, but it quickly becomes more stable when repeated in cycles 38 (beat 5), 39 (beat 4) and 40 (beats 1–3). Instability is encouraged because of the structure of the zither: without a string pitched to f, the e string is raised to f as tension is added by pressing beyond the bridge. From cycle 41, the character of this tone changes, and f becomes the higher acciaccatura to e (or e^b) as a breaking tone. This undermines *p'yŏngjo*. A hint of the falling motif in cycle 42, although transitory, further blurs the modal identity, and cycle 43 gives an ascending statement of the three characteristic *kyemyŏnjo* tones: g (sol), c (do), e–d (mi–re), the last given an extended portamento treatment known by musicians as '*yŏŭm*'. Cycle 44 adds a cadence, ending on c as the central tone: *kyemyŏnjo* has arrived. *Kyemyŏnjo* is explored in the sixth 'melody' (cycles 45–8) and, transposed down a fifth, in the seventh (cycles 49–60). With the seventh, the three characteristic tones are accorded careful and full treatment: the central tone (g) is given little vibrato, while the dominant (d) gets much more and the breaking tone (falling to a) is prominent. The treatment of the tonic begins to change in cycle 55, where g is approached from below and above, plucked with the soft fleshy part of the finger then with the nail. Cycle 57 suggests all is well, with concentration on d as the vibrated dominant, but cycle 59 shifts back to a central tone on c.

It would be prescient at this point to ask the extent to which Kim Chukp'a or other creators of *sanjo* were conscious of structure. If planning can be discerned to this point, the eighth, ninth and tenth 'melodies' (cycles 61–4, 65–76, 77–82) seem rather curious. They hesitate before settling on either c or g as the central tone, and shift from one to the other with little obvious cohesion. The murky waters suddenly become clear with 'melody' 11 (cycles 83–90). This constitutes something of an arrival, presenting an authentic *kyemyŏnjo* firmly rooted on c as the central tone. The pitch g is given constant and deep vibrato as the dominant, and the breaking-tone complexes utilize all semitones between f and d. *Kyemyŏnjo*, from a structural point of view, might be expected to run to the end of the movement, so as to give resolution and completion, but Kim Chukp'a has other ideas.

She uses 'melody' 11 to develop a climax that continues through 'melody' 12 (cycles 91–100) but with elements of reprise. Cycle 91 echoes cycle 23, the beginning of the third 'melody', but shifts the central tone up a fifth to g. What should now be the dominant, d, disappears, except for a single quaver following a portamento in beat 5 of cycle 94, which prevents any feeling of arrival. The last three beats of both cycles 92 and 93 give the new central tone, g, both with and without vibrato. However, the modal integrity of *kyemyŏnjo* is not threatened, since Kim is merely extending her notion of adding colour, this time from *ujo*. Indeed, beat 4 in cycle 95 reasserts *kyemyŏnjo*, preceded by strong octave repetitions of c played without vibrato: the central tone has fallen to c and settled. A final threat comes in cycle 99, where an echo of cycle 6 reasserts *ujo*, but the *kyemyŏnjo* 'breaking tones', 'vibrating tones', and the steady-pitched central tone all remain intact. A cadence ends the movement at cycle 100, vibrated dominants (g) resolving onto steady central tones (c). The final note, an e^b, joins *chinyangjo* to the beginning of *chungmori*, fusing the first and second movements together (this note would be omitted if a performer were to stop at this point).

Chungmori

In *p'ansori*, a single 12/4 cycle of *chungmori* forms a complete unit. The model pattern divides into four three-beat units, the first, second and fourth sometimes articulated with initial left-hand strikes on the drum, and the third almost always given with an accent on its third beat (the ninth crotchet in the 12/4 cycle). This last accent sets up the fourth three-beat unit as an elongated upbeat, returning us neatly to the beginning of the cycle. An appropriate balance between voice (or melodic instrument) and drum maintains tension, with space for breaths at the end of phrases – typically the end of cycles. The regularity means that *chungmori* is forgiving, and a novice can relatively easily maintain the accompaniment with little variation, but a melodic density rule applies: where the vocal or melodic instrument part is full the accompanist plays less, omitting parts of the model pattern, while when a melodic tone is sustained, or when the melody falls temporarily silent, a drummer needs to enhance his accompaniment. Similarly, when a melodic phrase continues from one cycle to the next, the accompanist should omit any cadential pattern.

Kim Tongjun matched Kim Chukp'a closely. This was more than a matter of balance. For example, in cycles 11 and 12, Kim Tongjun introduced double acciaccature and fast patterning as Kim Chukp'a explored a flowing quaver/eighth-note melody. The accompaniment to cycles 26–8 was particularly skilful, reducing the strike rate at first, then increasing it to echo Kim Chukp'a's repeating dotted crotchet+semiquaver+quaver melodic pattern across a falling second or third interval. Kim Tongjun picked up the melodic syncopation, as he also did in cycle 47, in a manner reminiscent of *ch'uimsae*, the 'shouts of encouragement' a drummer gives to a *p'ansori* singer in response to skilful manipulation of material. Kim Chukp'a used cadential patterns sparingly in her *chungmori* movement. Rather than pause, she generated pace at the end of cycles, continuing into the next to maintain melodic interest. Kim Tongjun followed her lead, and throughout the movement offered only two cadences. The first, in cycle 10, came as an instant response to a melodic cadential pattern ending with an octave g–g sustained over four beats. In verbal notation, it can be rendered as *kidok ttok ttokttok* (acciaccatura/crotchet+quaver+sem iquaver+semiquaver). The second cadence was at the very end of the movement, and was less complete, simply because Kim Chukp'a moved straight to the third movement, *chungjungmori*, without pause. Kim Tongjun only had one small hiccup: he ended cycle 5 poorly, giving a single strike on the final beat as the *kayagŭm* paused, where a cadential drum pattern, such as *ttong kidok ttok* (crotchet+acciaccatura/quaver+quaver) would have been more appropriate.

As Kim Chukp'a described it, there is a distinct feel of *kyŏngdŭrŭm* as the *chungmori* movement begins (Kim often referred to this as '*kyŏngjo*'). This is given by the repeated c played with octave acciaccature right at the start, then by the occasional use of a as a passing tone. The three sub-sections of the first 'melody' (cycles 1–7, 8–10 and 11–16) move progressively closer to *p'yŏngjo*, but in the first cycles, the pitch f is often replaced by e: both are outside the normative palette of *p'yŏngjo*. *Kyŏngdŭrŭm*, as noted above, is used in *p'ansori*; it is the 'quaint, unassuming, pure voice of a herd boy' (Yi Kukcha 1989: 200), the 'Seoul mode, the voice of political correctness' (Chan E. Park 2003: 182). In respect to the latter, the repeated octaves on c are spot on. The second 'melody', cycles 17–30, is reminiscent of the Kangsan school which, moving southwards from the capital of Seoul, is one stage closer to Chŏlla (and to *kyemyŏnjo*) and gives considerable and regular vibrato to the dominant, g. It initially avoids the breaking tone that would signal the arrival of *kyemyŏnjo*, but hints at it in cycles 24 and 25, with falling e–d, f–e^b, and e–c–d decorations; the hints become more substantial during cycles 26–8 with a series of syncopated gasps played as falling portamenti from e^b. Still, though, the feeling is brighter than the emotional intensity normative to *kyemyŏnjo*, although in the final two cycles a statement appears echoing the beginning of the movement but now clearly in *kyemyŏnjo*.

The third 'melody', starting in cycle 31, briefly takes us back to the beginning of *chinyangjo*, and to the *ujo* mode with which that movement began. To underline the mode, each of cycles 31–5 cadences on a (la) and intimates the falling motif of the 'Song of Chŏksŏng'. In cycle 35, there is a repeat of the melodic idea from cycle 4 of the *chinyangjo* movement, now an octave higher. Cycle 38 onwards, just as in the third 'melody' of the *chinyangjo* movement, begins to shift towards *kyemyŏnjo*, but a tone higher than might be expected. The central tone begins to shift to d in cycle 42, and a cadential hint comes in the last three-beat unit of cycle 44; this new central tone fully arrives by cycle 46, when a prominent and vibrated dominant, a, provides emphasis. But a bridge passage at the end of cycle 47 (again descending from the *chinyangjo* movement) deposes this central tone, shifting down a tone. We are now one stage closer to *kyemyŏnjo*, as the new dominant, g, is given with deep vibrato. The fourth 'melody', beginning in cycle 53, is in a fully fledged *kyemyŏnjo*, and maintains this mode to the end of the movement in cycle 64. Repeated central tones (c) are given very little ornamentation, unlike heavily vibrated dominants (g), while 'breaking tones' feature portamenti down to d or down from e^b.

Chungjungmori

The pace quickens at the beginning of the *chungjungmori* movement.[24] Because of this, novice accompanists tend to maintain constructs that barely depart from model patterns. Indeed, concentration is required: not only must the accompanist continue to anticipate the melodic instrument, providing constant balance, but melodic hemiola and syncopation add considerable complexity. Kim Chukp'a was renowned for adding a little rubato in a way that cut across metric regularity, particularly in the faster movements of *sanjo* (she regularly added rubato in cycle 3 of *chungjungmori* and cycle 2 of *chungmori*). Precisely because of this, the formidable Kim Myŏnghwan had more difficulty following her than Kim Tongjun. The latter was most familiar with her playing, since they were near neighbours and practised together regularly. Kim Myŏnghwan, though, knew Ham Tongjŏngwŏl's style of playing intimately, and was well able to handle her idiosyncrasies, whereas Kim Tongjun could not. In the days before Chaesuk Lee's notations, regularity was less of a concern to *sanjo* masters who, in the words of Lee Hye-ku, used 'artistic licence' (*yesuljŏgin och'a*).[25]

Familiarity with the Kim Chukp'a style is particularly crucial in her *chajinmori* movement, where the accompanist must respond to each melodic strand. Kim Tongjun does this in exemplary fashion from bar 25 onwards, where he first increases the strike rate to match ascending melodic figures, then offers an almost imperceptible repeating quaver pulse as the zither gallops along repeating a rhythmic filigree. As the second 'melody' begins in bar 34, marked by a 6/4 melody cutting across the 12/8 flow, the accompanist should drop all but the initial downbeat, so as not to disrupt matters; when 12/8 is restored in bar 57, the drummer needs to immediately reinstate fuller model patterns. Similarly, ostinato melodic patterns in the *hwimori* movement require soft accompaniment so as not to drown them out, while the *senza misura* section at that movement's end is routinely given with a relaxed accompaniment that repeats, at a distance, the basic model pattern without articulation. Again, in the final movement, *sesanjoshi*, the virtuosic speed and melodic intricacy of the zither demands little more than initial downbeats from the accompanist, or, sometimes, a drum strike only in every other bar. The drum is also required to drop out completely towards the end, as a final *senza misura* section balances the *tasŭrŭm* that introduced the whole performance, rejoining for a final triumphant cadence.

Ham Tongjŏngwŏl regarded her *chungjungmori* as being in *ujo* mode, but was alone in doing so. Others, including Kim Chukp'a, considered their *chungjungmori* movements as Kangsan school. The appropriate modal characteristics, then, are found in atmosphere and expression: brightness and clarity, with vibrato accorded the dominant in a manner somewhere between the Eastern and Western schools, without the pathos and sorrow associated with *kyemyŏnjo*. Within the 43 bars of her *chungjungmori* movement, however, Kim Chukp'a introduces both *p'yŏngjo* and *kyemyŏnjo* elements. In the first bar, the dominant (g) is given prominent vibrato, but in bar 2 what should be the lower part of a breaking tone (d) is repeated without any

---

[24]   Hence, for clarity, what we have so far called 'cycles' will henceforth be referred to as 'bars'.

[25]   This is one element in the (re)development of a performance aesthetic that has been discussed by Korean musicologists since the mid-1990s. See, in English, Lee Byong Won (1997, 1999).

portamento or acciaccatura; in bars 4, 6, 8, 9 and 10 an acciaccatura leads up to the lower part of the breaking tone rather than falling to it. A shift up a tone begins in bar 9, increasing the *p'yŏngjo* feel, enhancing this by a characteristic *p'yŏngjo* falling motif at the end of bar 10. The *p'yŏngjo* ascending scale is outlined in bar 13, by which time typical *p'yŏngjo* progressions previously heard in the fifth 'melody' of *chinyangjo* are reprised. The appearance of the tone e from bar 20 onwards moves away from *p'yŏngjo*, and with falling portamenti to e from above in bars 21 and 23, hints of the breaking tone of *kyemyŏnjo* reappear. Note that two breaking-tone pitch complexes are used (the upper tone being higher than f in one case), both played on the zither's seventh string with an initial stretching of the string beyond the movable bridge. In bar 29, the eighth string (tuned to f) substitutes for the seventh, essentially reintroducing the *p'yŏngjo* feel. A further detour towards *kyemyŏnjo* waylays us in bars 35–6.

Chajinmori

The bulk of Kim's *chajinmori* movement – the first, second, fourth and fifth 'melodies' (bars 1–33, 34–44, 64–71 and 72–80) – is cast in solid *kyemyŏnjo*. The central tone is emphasized at length at the beginning, with octave displacements, but, although 'breaking tones' appear as the melodic contour expands from bar 10 onwards, only limited vibrato is accorded the dominant. The first 'melody' is lengthy, and a cadence pattern set up in bar 31 is repeated several times before finally leading to the second 'melody'. We cast off on a new tack, in 6/4 metre, although the cadence that comes in bars 43–4 resembles that of bar 31. The third 'melody' shifts to *ujo* by raising the central tone up one tone. The initial statement (bar 45) functions as a bridge and is atypical, but bars 51, 53, 55 and 57 hark back to the falling 'Song of Chŏksŏng' motif. The cadence idea returns in bar 63, now played a tone higher, introducing an extension of the melody that adds occasional 'breaking tones' as a gradual modulation takes us down a tone back towards *kyemyŏnjo*; this, Chaesuk Lee considers, signifies the Kangsan school. The fourth and fifth 'melodies' form a mirror to the opening, repeating the cadential pattern and emphasizing the central tone through octave dispositions.

Hwimori

The *hwimori* movement is in *kyemyŏnjo* throughout, as if the rapid pace discourages anything that might signal modulation. When Kim Chukp'a taught Chaesuk Lee in the late 1960s, she did not divide *hwimori* from *chajinmori*, saying that it had been the custom of her primary teacher, Han Sŏnggi, to fuse the two together. Similarly, Sŏng Kŭmyŏn resisted dividing the two, and Ham Tongjŏngwŏl simply divided them into slow (*nŭjin*) *chajinmori* and *chajinmori* proper. Kim split them into two movements in the 1970s, perhaps influenced by Kim Yundŏk's practice. The latter was already a holder of the Intangible Cultural Property, and Kim Chukp'a was preparing for nomination. She added considerable new material, and by the late 1970s divided the movement into six 'melodies' (bars 1–35, 36–53, 54–88, 89–108, 109–23 and 124–45), with an additional free rhythm section to conclude. Of these, the second, fourth and fifth were new. The free rhythm section consists of seven phrases of different lengths, the first four predating the 1970s. It is customary for the accompanist to softly provide a constant repetition of the model rhythmic cycle as a ground throughout this section, although, as with the opening *tasŭrŭm*, the zither melody avoids any sense of pulse.

Sesanjoshi

The final movement continues in the same vein, albeit at an even more cracking pace. Solid *kyemyŏnjo* rules the first four 'melodies' (bars 1–36, 37–54, 55–96 and 97–135). The first sets up a characteristic quaver motif (g–g–g–d–g) that in the second is inverted and developed (to c–c–c–d–g, g–g–g–e–f, and so on). The third fuses this to a cadence from the *chajinmori* movement and octave displacement, providing an ostinato that is carried through to the fourth 'melody'. The fifth (bars 136–76) allows both zither and drum to catch breath, shifting the central tone up a fifth (to g), and adding vibrato to the new dominant (d). Elements of the quaver motif regularly recur, and in bar 161 the central tone begins to fall back to c, although the feeling is Kangsan school rather than *kyemyŏnjo*, since there is little sense of vibrated dominants or breaking tones. The final free rhythm section, until the 1970s a single phrase but from then onwards recast as three drawn-out phrases, pulls us back, mirroring the very opening of the introduction, but through calmness and clarity reflecting the Kangsan style.

Concluding Remarks

Many musicologists and ethnomusicologists have written extensively on the characteristics of Korean music. This is not surprising, since such accounts go someway to satisfy a common question: 'what is special about Korean music?' Such writings characterize a period in ethnomusicology, a style, and a way of doing things. They should have been superseded several decades ago as scholars became more reflexive, as the paradigm of fieldwork spread, and as critiques of the concept of culture led to what Timothy Rice (2003: 156) calls 'subject-centred musical ethnography'.[26] Nonetheless, requests for pithy explanations of difference continue, for ethnomusicologists being the inheritance of our *Musikwissenschaft* forebears, and in Korea tied closely to concepts of identity.[27]

---

[26] Rice summarizes far more than these critiques, assessing Arjun Appadurai's concept of 'deterritorialization', James Clifford's comment about continuities between pasts and presents, and Veit Erlmann's observation that 'accounting for a world system of global/local dialectics and accounting for the experience of that system … are not the same' (Rice 2003: 152–6).

[27] Studies of Korean culture (*Han'guk munhwaron*) and Korean race (*Han'guginnon*) are widely promoted within Korea. Amongst them, the publications of Ch'oe Ch'unshik (for example, Ch'oe 1997, 2000), the three books on Korean heritage by Yu Hongjun that have sold in excess of a million copies (Yu 1993–1997), and the more than 100 volumes by Yi Kyut'ae may be considered representative. Such publications tend to describe shared value systems that are unique and unitary, and find 'ways of thinking which dominate and determine every behavior and feature of Koreans who are different from foreigners' (Yi Kyut'ae 1983, as translated and cited in Kweon Sug-In 2003: 46).

There remain differences in the accounts of foreigners (who mostly accept their designation as 'ethnomusicologists') and Korean scholars (who are more likely to refer to themselves as 'musicologists').[28] Howard's earlier publications, for example, have explored melodic contour, ornamentation and rhythmic constructs as basic building blocks. In contrast, Korean scholars delineate mode as a primary characteristic. In this, they follow conventions set out by the founder of Korean musicology, Lee Hye-ku (see Howard 2002). Mode is often extracted from notation; mode is used to define regional folksong styles, much as if a linguistic dialect (Han Manyŏng 1972, 1973, 1974); seven modes are distinguished in *p'ansori* (Paek 1982; Um 1992; Park 2003). However, the rationale for proposing mode as primary differentiates musicological discourse from much contemporary ethnomusicology, and indeed from the work of anthropologists and folklorists. Why should the average itinerant musician, who until recent times learnt court or folk music by rote and without notation, be concerned with the abstractions that constitute mode?

Howard, as the ethnomusicologist, began this project believing that the dialect of *sanjo* needed to be conceived of as a mix of mode, rhythm and pitch treatment, all influenced by the physical and acoustic properties of the melodic instrument – no longer, though, since the analysis above has confirmed the Korean musicological perspective. With one possible exception, the brief motif reminiscent of the 'Song of Chŏksŏng', the melodic material of *sanjo* does not quote specific *p'ansori* or folksong repertory. It does, however, explore carefully conceived and worked-out modal structures, all of which have parallels with, and at times seem to be inspired by, the vocal acrobatics of *p'ansori* singers. Beyond this, individual melodic phrases are in *sanjo* knitted together to create what Kim Chukp'a referred to as 'melodies' and these extended ideas, while ideally suited to a melodic instrument, are far removed from vocal text-based phrasing. 'Melodies' always remain faithful to model rhythmic cycles, *changdan*, but they do so framed by the three core modes – *kyemyŏnjo*, *ujo*, *p'yŏngjo* – and the different singing styles of *p'ansori*. Mode, then, is a basic building block, but is it the primary building block? We would still like to conceive of *sanjo* in a different way, asking how motifs build to melodic strands, and how motivic material underpins structure, and this, using a very different approach, is precisely what we attempt in Chapter 5.

---

[28] The distinction is made by Hwang Jun-yon (1998: v).

Chapter 5

Analysis 2:
A Deleuzian Approach

> It is as though an immense plane of consistency of variable speed were forever sweeping up forms and functions, forms and subjects, extracting from them particles and affects. A clock keeping up a whole assortment of time. (Deleuze and Guattari 1987: 271)

The most clearly defined explication of Deleuze and Guattari's thinking on music can be found in plateaus ten and eleven of *A Thousand Plateaus*, from which the above quote is taken. Although the borders of musical reference are limited, the conceptual framework which Deleuze and Guattari provide (1977) has proved useful in discussions of a wide range of musical activity, such as can be seen in the recent *Deleuze on Music*, where Boulez, the Maori *haka*, Miles Davis, and Death, Doom and Black Metal are all deliberated (Buchanan and Swiboda 2004). It would not seem without reason, then, that the concepts contained within Deleuze and Guattari's writings about music may be useful in developing an interpretative framework for Kim Chukp'a's *sanjo*, particularly since reference is given on a number of occasions to Eastern concepts of musical time and form.

In bringing this framework to bear *on sanjo*, we note again the potential or real clash between ethnomusicological and Korean musicological approaches that we have identified in Chapter 4. To help resolve this clash, and in order for the dialogue of *sanjo* to develop advantageously, we consider it useful to adopt an interpretative framework that originated outside that of the purely musical domain. This framework should not restrict itself to the purely 'Korean' aspects of the music (however Koreanness is defined). Such a framework is doubly important taking into account that Korean musicology has developed considerably since the mid-twentieth century, employing a number of analytical techniques for *sanjo* and other genres of Korean music that have allowed it to reach, but in a sense that is different to that used by Deleuze and Guattari, a plateau of its own. How can this plateau be aligned to different philosophical and academic traditions? To answer this, Chapter 5 draws on a number of analytical techniques developed both in Korea and in the Western academy at the same time as being framed by Deleuze and Guattari. Our aim is to move away from a primary focus on mode to allow fruitful comparison of the ways in which various melodies are re-articulated through rhythm during the course of performance. We argue that *sanjo* is formed from the articulation of a small number of melodic strands that recur in a number of movements with different rhythmic articulation, proceeding by way of involution, whereby the pitch content of strands is gradually reduced to an alternation between the tonic and dominant of (primarily) *kyemyŏnjo* mode. To do so, we use a number of Deleuzian[1] concepts and ideas with the hope that this will allow for further possibilities of interpretation and discussion of what is an extremely temporally complex and intriguing musical form.

Our collaboration was of paramount importance in the development of this account, and it is primarily through the transcription of Chaesuk Lee that a second level of interpretation, made following her studies with Kim Chukp'a, has occurred. There is always the risk of sophistry when appropriating ideas developed in a different cultural tradition, though we would argue that in this case a number of key concepts such as 'speed' and 'movement', 'pulsed time' and 'non-pulsed time', which in themselves are quite general, can cross the divide as they detail temporal processes that occur in music regardless of its cultural origin. Our collaboration, in respect to this chapter, gave the opportunity for discussion between a leading Korean performer of the genre and a British composer/musicologist, with the concepts detailed below being tested for validity and relevance. This was very much a two-way process whereby the composer/musicologist offered ideas and observations about *kayagŭm sanjo*, which the performer interrogated for appropriateness, then responded with ideas and suggestions that, in turn, influenced the composer/musicologist. Such interaction did not have the requirement of anthropological rigour, since it was less a discussion of social context than an elucidation of musical processes, underpinned by a philosophical interpretation. It may be seen as distant from more usual ethnomusicological practice, since it allows *sanjo* to be placed in a wider context than when confined to issues relating to the genre's historical and cultural development.

Kim Chukp'a's *sanjo* was, until brought within Korean musicological discourse (both for analysis and for learning and practice by students studying for degrees), to an extent improvisatory, but here we use Chaesuk Lee's transcription as our primary source. However, our account remains an account of performance practice. A transcription may help to locate particular musical gestures at certain moments in time and allow comparative judgements to be made with justification from the score, but the overall process of making, creating and recreating music can still be defined using the concepts detailed below. Similarly, as discussed in earlier chapters, *sanjo* allows for different performance lengths, but regardless of the length of performance the interaction of mode, rhythm and articulation – the techniques of vibrato, string-bending and glissando introduced in Chapter 2 – all proceed in ways that can be defined using a Deleuzian philosophical approach.

We first define a number of key concepts that Deleuze uses in his description of music which are of relevance, to enable their relation to the music itself – which will be discussed in a second part – to become apparent. Deleuze's explication of these concepts in *A Thousand Plateaus* does not enable pithy description, as throughout his book they are regularly placed in different contexts, being constantly

---

[1]   In this chapter, for expediency, we will use 'Deleuzian' and its derivatives rather than 'Deleuzian and Guattarian', as has been done by a number of others. Felix Guattari worked with Deleuze on *A Thousand Plateaus* and also on *Anti-Oedipus*, the first part of the combined work subtitled *Capitalism and Schizophrenia*. However, Deleuze's philosophical output is contained within a larger volume of work, which was influential in the development of the conceptual framework for *Capitalism and Schizophrenia*.

'deterritorialized' (to use his own terminology). Indeed, Brian Massumi writes in the introduction to *A Thousand Plateaus* that Deleuze's thought 'replaces the closed equation of representation, $x = x =$ not y with the open equation of $... + y + z + a$. Rather than analysing the world into discrete components, reducing their manyness to the One of Identity, and ordering them by rank ... it synthesizes a multiplicity of elements without effacing their heterogeneity or hindering their potential for future rearranging' (Deleuze and Guattari 1987: xiii). The placement of concepts in different contexts denies their reduction to the 'One of Identity'. As will be seen below, this compares with the way in which *sanjo* proceeds during performance, with the constant re-articulation of melody through rhythm.

Deleuze's discussion of music offers important concepts for the interpretation of *kayagŭm sanjo* of the 'milieu' and its interaction with rhythm, 'territories' and 'assemblages', and the 'deterritorialization' of the refrain. Each of these concepts works in conjunction to enable a complex interaction of ideas that elucidates the way in which *sanjo* unfolds over time.[2] Similarly, the notion of speed, contained within the concept of the 'plane of consistency', as contextualized in the quote at the beginning of this chapter, also plays a relevant part, particularly considering the distinction made between pulsed and non-pulsed time that is key to *sanjo*. Although Deleuze does not consider 'involution' an essential philosophical concept, though of significance, it highlights an important process that occurs during performance, and in the following pages will be used to underpin other concepts.

Milieu and Rhythm

In French, 'milieu' has three different meanings: 'surroundings', 'medium' (as in chemical agency) and 'middle'. Deleuze uses a combination of all three (Massumi 1987: xvii). The chemical reference, whereby milieu can be seen as a substance through which a force or other influence is transmitted – the analogy of a seed and a crystalline solution is used by Ian Buchanan in his introduction to *Deleuze on Music* (Buchanan and Swiboda 2004: 9) – is particularly appropriate considering the fluidity of the concept and the way in which milieus interact in a constant network of exchange and affect. As Deleuze writes in the eleventh *plateau*:

> Every milieu is coded, a code being defined by periodic repetition; but each code is in a perpetual state of transcoding or transduction. Transcoding or transduction is the manner in which one milieu serves as the basis for another, or conversely is established atop another milieu, dissipates in it or is constituted in it. The notion of the milieu is

---

2   In the conclusion to *A Thousand Plateaus*, Deleuze and Guattari specify six essential concepts: strata and stratification, assemblages, rhizome, plane of consistency (body without organs), deterritorialization, and abstract machines (diagram and phylum). All other concepts are considered as subsets of these (Deleuze and Guattari 1987: 502–14). The critical evaluation of all these concepts lies outside the scope of this chapter. The use of the key ideas above is considered particularly relevant to sanjo, and will be discussed within a musical context. For a particularly insightful critique of Deleuze's writings about music see Ronald Bogue (2004), and for a wider interpretation of Deleuze's earlier work see Eugene W. Holland (1999).

not unitary: not only does the living thing continually pass into one another; they are essentially communicating. (Deleuze and Guattari 1987: 313)

It is easy to relate the notion of code to mode, with different milieus being viewed as different modes. A single change in pitch of one note in the mode results in the formation of a new mode, so, for example, a change from f to f# in C major results in a shift to G major. In this sense, the notion of transcoding or transduction, as 'the manner in which one milieu serves as the basis for another', is appropriate. However, at a more molecular level, the articulatory forces that act upon a particular sound, including vibrato, bending the pitch and glissando, play a much more prominent role in Korean music performance than in much Western music, and can also be defined by the milieu. These different articulations interact with the modes that constitute sanjo, and thus an analysis of the interaction is needed.

Deleuze further categorizes milieu using four spatial locators, in keeping with his hypothesis that every 'milieu is ... a block of space-time' (Deleuze and Guattari 1987: 313). The sub-milieus comprise an 'interior milieu of composing subjects', an 'exterior milieu of materials', an 'intermediary milieu of membranes and limits', and an 'annexed milieu of energy sources'. The sub-milieus have been defined in less abstract terms, though with analogies given by Deleuze in *A Thousand Plateaus*, by Ronald Bogue (2003). For Bogue, they can be described in relation to an amoeba's milieu, its surrounding liquid medium acting as the external milieu, its organs as the internal milieu,[3] its exchange across the cell membrane as the intermediary milieu, and the annexed milieu being defined by the organism's relation to food, sunlight and other sources of energy (Bogue 2003: 17–18). Sub-milieus interact with each other causing, in certain conditions such as the processing of food, a change in cell shape. To use a musical analogy that can be related to *sanjo*, the interior milieu could be perceived of as the actual sound of a particular string on the zither, with the material of the string (silk) acting as the exterior milieu. The instrument itself acts as the intermediary milieu, the limit placed upon the string in terms of tension and resulting pitch. The annexed milieu is the force of the fingers, the source of energy that allows the string to sound, whether plucked or flicked with the fingers of the right hand, with vibrato achieved by an oscillating movement of the left hand.[4]

Milieu, as a 'block of space-time constituted by the periodic repetition of the component' (Deleuze and Guattari 1987: 313), has a symbiotic relationship with rhythm. A distinction should be made, however, between periodic repetition defined as a measure or metre, the continual repetition of the same, and rhythm proper, which exists in the in-between, the transcoded space between two milieus:

---

[3]   Bogue does not clarify his use of 'organs': an amoeba, as a single cell animal, does not have organs in the usual sense of the word.

[4]   Buchanan describes milieu in less microscopic terms in his introduction to *Deleuze on Music*. There, the exterior milieu is the way in which a particular movement of a person's head, a smile or a laugh, sets them apart from a crowd, while the interior milieu is what lies beneath that smile. Buchanan is not clear in his description of intermediary and annexed milieus, but it can be deduced that the former has a regulatory function that allows or disallows certain social interactions, with the latter comprises sources of energy, the sensory and emotional facilities that enable interaction to occur and, through time, change.

Metre, whether regular or not, assumes a coded form whose unit of measure may vary, but in a noncommunicating milieu, whereas rhythm is the Unequal or the Incommensurable that is always undergoing transcoding. Rhythm ... ties itself together in passing from one milieu to another. It does not operate in a homogeneous space-time, but by heterogeneous blocks. (Deleuze and Guattari 1987: 313)

Messiaen is given as a rhythmic composer of exemplary standing in *A Thousand Plateaus*, as a musician whose use of rhythm works in the space 'in-between' the even and uniform division of time created by metre. The most important of Messiaen's rhythmic techniques are said to be added values, the related rhythmic characters, and non-retrogradable rhythms. Added values are processes in which short durations, typically a semiquaver that can be an additional note, rest or dot, are added to a rhythmic line, whose underlying metre without such an additional duration would be explicit. By such a process, a simple 2/4 metre, for example, can become the more complex 9/16 metre. 'When employed frequently in a composition, added values undermine all metrical regularity, and the bar lines, rather than marking fixed units of time, demarcate rhythmic cells of varying duration' (Bogue 2003: 26).[5] The added value, in the context of the milieu, is the transcoding element that allows for this in-between rhythmical time to become actual, and it is the continual interaction between the added value and a milieus periodic repetition or metre that is rhythmical.[6]

How can one proclaim the constituent inequality of rhythm while at the same time admitting implied vibrations, periodic repetitions of components? A milieu does in fact exist by virtue of a periodic repetition, but one whose only effect is to produce a difference by which the milieu passes into another milieu. It is the difference that is rhythmic, not the repetition. (Deleuze and Guattari 1987: 313)

In contrast to the metrically demarcated and measured time that situates a regulated succession of past, present and future which Deleuze calls *Chronos* there is a 'free-floating' time, achieved through the complete cessation of metre, which Deleuze calls '*Aeon*', 'the indefinite time of the event, the floating line that knows only speeds' (Deleuze and Guattari 1987: 262). He relates *Chronos* and *Aeon* with Pierre Boulez's (1971) distinction between pulsed and non-pulsed time, the latter not organized in relation to any external and periodic repetition but which 'has nothing but speeds' (Deleuze and Guattari 1987: 262).[7]

---

[5]   See Bogue (2003: 24–31) for an explanation of Messiaen's rhythmic techniques. The description of added values is taken from Messiaen's *Technique de mon langage musical* (1944).

[6]   Another composer who developed a rhythmic process that allows for in-between time to become actual is Elliott Carter. A number of his compositions use 'tempo modulation', a procedure whereby a division of the pulse of one tempo becomes the pulse of another. See David Schiff (1983) for a detailed discussion.

[7]   Bogue, in *Deleuze's Wake*, draws attention to the difference between Boulez's and Deleuze's categorization of speed (2004: 96). For Deleuze, only non-pulsed music 'has nothing but speeds' whilst, for Boulez, speed is explicitly tied to pulsed time. Bogue cites Boulez's comment: 'Only pulsed time is susceptible to speed, acceleration or deceleration: the regular or irregular referential system on which it is based is a function of a chronometric time

Speed is not an organizational principle as such, although the metrical time of *Chronos* arguably is, but an affect that passes across events, a process in a continual state of becoming. This state, which Deleuze associates within the 'plane of consistency', does not produce 'forms or developments of forms' but is concerned only with 'relations of movement and rest, speed and slowness between unformed elements, or at least between elements that are relatively unformed' (Deleuze and Guattari 1987: 262). This contrasts with the formal procedures of much Western art music – symphonies, for example – based upon developmental processes, and which Deleuze associates with the 'plane of organization'. However, in a similar way to how the sub-milieus interact with each other, the plane of organization and the plane of consistency, although seen as two abstract poles, draw differing degrees of intensity from one another:

> [The] plane of consistency is constantly extricating itself from the plane of organization, causing particles to spin off the strata, scrambling forms by dint of speed and slowness, breaking down functions by means of assemblages or micro-assemblages. (Deleuze and Guattari 1987: 270)

In keeping with the nature of Deleuze's thinking, milieu is not given any fixed meaning, which would act as a ground, as meaning is variable depending upon context, with all variations and interactions giving rise to new possibilities that in turn influence each other. In Kim Chukp'a's *sanjo*, certain articulative procedures, such as the strength of vibrato and pitch inflections associated with certain modes, are transferred, or established on top, constituted in other modes influencing, and in the sense used by Deleuze, communicating with them. Similarly, as we have shown in Chapter 4, the demarcation of time is in a constant state of flux with differing metrical divisions enabling a constant re-articulation of melody. Both categories of time, pulsed and non-pulsed, exist within *sanjo*, with the overall process of acceleration, a category of speed, influencing the music at a deeper structural level. Thus, the abstract poles of the plane of organization and the plane of consistency are themselves in a continual process of interaction, enabling a highly complex delineation of time.

'Territories' and 'Assemblages'

Milieu is inclusive of territory, the process whereby milieu components, through ceasing to be directional and functional, become dimensional and expressive. Deleuze uses a number of biological analogies to explain this. The change in colour of tropical fish relates to an interior hormonal change that occurs when there is an external threat or other change in circumstance; it is functional and transitory. We can relate this to the various sub-milieus, the 'intermediary milieu of membranes and limits', for example, being the colour membrane of the fish. However, when colour, which can also act as a marker, acquires a temporal constancy and demonstrates a relation to a given space, it is territorial. For Deleuze, it becomes expressive. 'Expressiveness

---

of a greater or lesser delimitation, breadth or variability. The relationship of chronometric time to the number of pulsations will be the index of speed.'

is not reducible to the immediate effects of an impulse triggering an action in a milieu' (Deleuze and Guattari 1987: 317) as it would be with the change in colour of tropical fish. Rather, 'expressive qualities find an objectivity in the territory they draw' (Deleuze and Guattari 1987: 317). To relate the notion of territory to music, the metre of a rhythmic cycle (of which there are a number in *sanjo*) would be considered functional rather than expressive, a milieu rather than a territory. It is the interaction of rhythm with this underlying metre that enables expression to become manifest. Hence, '[t]erritorialization is an act of rhythm that has become expressive, or of milieu components that have become qualitative. The marking of a territory is dimensional, but it is not metre, it is rhythm' (Deleuze and Guattari 1987: 315).

The categorization of mode or scale within this conceptual framework is complicated because pitch relies on rhythm for its articulation. Mode without rhythm can only exist as an abstract entity; rhythm and temporal intervals make it manifest. As soon as one pitch of a mode moves to another, a temporal interval is formed, with each further pitch movement marking another temporal interval. In addition, temporal intervals can be organized within a metre – the pulsed time of *Chronos* – or alternatively can remain outside any such periodic repetition, existing in the non-pulsed time of *Aeon*. This, however, is not the only agency that acts upon a pitch. Articulative forces, in addition to dynamics, that act upon a sound in *kayagŭm sanjo* are also implicated, namely vibrato, pitch bending and glissando. These combine with rhythm to create a complex interaction of milieus and territories through which articulation becomes expressive. In Deleuzian terms, expressive 'qualities or matters of expression enter shifting relations with one another that "express" the relation of the territory they draw to the interior milieu of impulses and the exterior milieu of circumstances' (Deleuze and Guattari 1987: 317).

The combination of metre, rhythm, articulation, mode and melody draws attention to the notion of the 'assemblage', which by definition is a conglomerate or an aggregate. The term used here is a translation of the French *agencement*, which, J. Macgregor Wise writes in *Gilles Deleuze: Key Concepts*, 'is not a static term; it is not the *arrangement* or *organization* but the process of arranging, organizing, fitting together' (in Stivale 2005: 77). It combines a variety of milieu and territories, a territorial assemblage, which possess the potential for a wider variety of expression. As we show in relation to *kayagŭm sanjo* below, through an interactive process with metre and rhythm, melody becomes expressive in a number of ways, the simplest being the differences in speed and rhythmic articulation that transverse each particular melody in each movement. Assemblages also operate in the space where milieus become decoded, 'extracting a territory from the milieus' (Deleuze and Guattari 1987: 503). Holland writes that decoding 'does not refer to the process of translating a secret meaning or message into a clearer form: on the contrary it refers to a process of dis-investing given meanings altogether, to a process of "uncoding," if you like: the destabilization and ultimately the elimination of established codes that confer fixed meaning' (Holland 1999: 20). Particular melodies are thus articulated in a variety of different ways, both within and across movements, denying the establishment of the fixed coding of a particular melody. We argue that this is taken to the extreme whereby the pitch content of a particular melody is reduced to primarily the tonic of the mode. This process is two-fold in that it denies the fixed coding of melody but also destabilizes the mode itself.

'Deterritorialization of the Refrain' and the Concept of 'Involution'

Deleuze describes music as the 'active, creative operation that consists of deterritorializing the refrain' (Deleuze and Guattari 1987: 300).[8] Musical refrains, he later notes, also have time-honoured associations with territoriality. To highlight this, he cites ancient Greek modes and the 'hundred rhythms' of the Hindu *devi talas* that are associated with specific regions or provinces. Deleuze also considers musical refrains to resemble birdsong, whose basic components delineate territories. 'Abstracting from these instances of geographically associated sonic motifs', he extends 'the notion of the refrain to refer to any kind of rhythmic or melodic pattern that stakes out a territory' (Bogue 2003: 16–17). The process through which a refrain is deterritorialized is essentially one of becoming, a passage between milieus and territories, with music 'making of the refrain a deterritorialized content for a deterritorializing form of expression' (Deleuze and Guattari 1987: 300).

To clarify this, Deleuze again refers to Messiaen, in particular to Messiaen's *Catalogue d'oiseaux*, the collection for solo piano portraying specific birds. However, in translating a particular birdsong, one finds that at every stage a deformation and mutation of the original takes place. As Bogue writes, 'the musical "translation" of an individual bird's song … deforms the song and renders it Other. And when one turns to the actual compositions that utilize birdsong, one encounters further forces of mutation and transformation that modify the sounds of nature' (Bogue 2003: 30). Similarily, deterritorialization of the refrain occurs in *kayagŭm sanjo*. Particular melodies are formed from specific modes which, as we noted in earlier chapters, can be associated with particular Korean geographical areas, but which also act as a refrain in the Deleuzian sense. These are dispersed throughout a performance, and are constantly transformed and mutated through metre and rhythmic articulation. Although there is proliferation of material within and across movements, 'this proliferation … has nothing to do with an evolution, the development of form or the filiation of form … It is, on the contrary, an involution, in which form is constantly being dissolved, freeing times and speeds' (Deleuze and Guattari 1987: 267).

The notion of involution is categorized in the 'plane of consistency' (discussed above). Such a plane, to quote again, does not produce 'forms or developments of forms', but is concerned with 'relations of movement and rest, speed and slowness between unformed elements, or at least between elements that are relatively unformed' (Deleuze and Guattari 1987: 262). Non-developmental processes contrast Western art music, which Deleuze places in the 'plane of organization'. The attraction of Western music towards this plane is not an absolute principle but one which Deleuze considers has dominated all Western classical music and continues to do so in European composition (Deleuze and Guattari 1987: 267). Greg Hainge considers that 'even when Western music is embarked upon a process of involution' – although no examples are offered – 'in which form is constantly being dissolved', there is always a concomitant development of form drawing it towards a plane of organization. This may be due in part to the reliance on a regular, pulsed metre that grounds it in *Chronos*

---

[8]   This is clearly a very different concept to that popularized by Arjun Appadurai (for example, 1996).

(Hainge, in Buchanan and Swiboda 2004: 39).[9] At this point, it is worth reporting responses to a questionnaire survey conducted in Korea in 1990 by Howard, reported in his *Preserving Korean Music* (2006). When respondents were asked what they liked about *kugak*, traditional Korean music, typical comments were: '*Kugak* leads us to examine our inner feelings'; 'Koreans alone can appreciate *kugak*'; '*Kugak* is owned by all Koreans'; '*Kugak* captures the essence of Korea, for Korean musicians are sensitive to the ways of our people'. However, the same question asked about Western art music elicited contrasting responses: 'My major was Western music, so I understand it and find it interesting'; 'European art music has the highest watermark'; 'The strength of Western music is its composition and order'.

Involution is associated with becoming, the 'domain of symbioses' which, as the plural suggests, should be seen more as an alliance of different elements that 'bring into play beings of totally different scales and kingdoms, with no possible filiation' (Deleuze and Guattari 1987: 238) than the hereditary process of evolution. The biological reference of symbiosis as the situation in which two different organisms live with and are dependent on each other is apt. Deleuze's philosophical approach distinguishes a number of elements, and it is the way that these interact and combine that allows for becoming and deterritorialization. The term involution does not refer to a process of regression: '[b]ecoming is involutionary, involution is creative. To regress is to move in the direction of something less differentiated. But to involve is to form a block that runs its own line "between" the terms in play and beneath assignable relations' (Deleuze and Guattari 1987: 238–9). And it is the interaction between rhythm, articulation, pitch and melody – the 'terms in play', of *kayagŭm sanjo*, and the process whereby a particular pitch gradually becomes more differentiated – to which we now turn.

We focus on specific aspects of *kayagŭm sanjo*: rhythm and rhythmic cycles, pitch, melody and articulation, guiding readers to examples in the transcription. This discussion, unlike Chapter 4, is not meant to be a descriptive analysis, but aims to move discussion beyond mode, relating the musical processes of *sanjo* to some of the philosophical concepts used by Deleuze, and demonstrating the overall delineation of *sanjo*, whereby, and as already indicated, a small number of melodic strands are constantly decoded or deterritorialized as performance progresses, resulting in a process of differentiation and involution.

Rhythm and Rhythmic Cycles

Six of the seven movements that constitute Kim Chukp'a's *kayagŭm sanjo* use a corresponding rhythmic cycle, maintained by the accompanying *changgo* drum. As can be seen from the cycles given in the transcription, and also from Notation 4.1, there is a diminution in the length of each cycle, resulting in an overall acceleration through the piece. It is of interest that in performance, in contrast to the explicit statements in much Western music ranging from Dunstaple's isorhythmic motets to the use of

---

9   Needless to say, the music of the twentieth century and much recent contemporary music can be interpreted as a reaction against such periodic repetition. Even in minimalist works such as Steve Reich's *Piano Phase* (for which, see Keith Potter's *Four Musical Minimalists* (2002)), metre is ambiguous.

rhythmic cycles in Ligeti's Piano Concerto, the rhythmic cycles in *kayagŭm sanjo* are often implicit. The skilled accompanist draws upon these coded units, keeping to the underlying strong and weak accents of each while articulating elements of the melody.

The interaction between rhythm in performance and the coded unit of a rhythmic cycle highlights the relationship between Deleuze's concept of the milieu and the 'periodic repetition of the component', the component here being the actual cycle. Through the interaction of the player with a cycle, each rhythmic code is in a 'perpetual state of transcoding'. In Chapter 4, we noted that in the *chungmori* movement the cycle is forgiving, and a novice can relatively easily maintain the accompaniment with little variation. To do so, though, would create little interest, because the rhythmic code would be functional, a model, the exact repetition instilling boredom. It is only through the interaction of rhythm proper in respect to the *kayagŭm* melody that a rhythmic cycle becomes expressive. This transcoding element generates interest, or expressiveness in the Deleuzian sense. In addition, depending on the experience of the player, balancing the cycle with the melody, with its process of tension and relaxation, can suffer.

The relationship between the accompanist, the rhythmic cycle, and the *kayagŭm* player is given expression throughout a *sanjo* performance through a network of exchange. This is not the only way in which rhythm works within the codified space of a rhythmic cycle, since the rhythmic articulation of melodies themselves, the complexity of a melodic instrument's interaction with a particular cycle being more intricate than that of the drum, is also involved. However, at most points in the course of performance melodies work within a codified space – the 18/8 metre of the *chinyangjo* movement, for example.

There is another temporal process that occurs at a deeper structural level, which conveys Deleuze's concepts of *Chronos* and *Aeon*. This is the relationship that rhythmic cycles have with *senza misura* sections – the *tasŭrŭm* movement that opens the work, the section near the end of the *hwimori* movement, and the conclusion to the *sesanjoshi* movement.[10] Deleuze defines *Chronos* as metrically demarcated time that has a regulated temporal succession, whereas *Aeon* is 'the floating line that knows only speeds'. It is the presence of both types of time, and the relationship between the two, that makes *sanjo* so temporally complex and intriguing.

The reductive principle in the cycles discussed in Chapter 4, combined with an increase in tempo, allows for acceleration in the music. Acceleration becomes manifest through pulse, the presence of which arguably becomes more ambiguous as the music progresses. The compound time *chinyangjo* movement has the slowest pulse. This comment, though, needs elaboration. Chaesuk Lee notes that her students often feel the underlying beat of the *chinyangjo* movement is faster than that of the *chungmori* cycle. The reason is that students tend to divide the *chinyangjo* beat into three – a dotted crotchet/eighth note divided into three quavers, the quaver being felt

---

[10]   Although it has been noted by Richard Widdess (1994: 62) that an implicit pulse is present in the *alap* section of a *dhrupad* performance which, formerly, had been considered to be performed without reference to a pulse, this is not the case with sanjo. In addition, Chaesuk Lee confirms that the non-pulsed *tasŭrŭm* movement is the last to be learnt, in the belief that it is only after a student has learnt the metrically demarcated music that they are able to fully and effectively interpret this movement.

as the pulse. However, Lee and other performers regard each dotted crochet/eighth note as one pulse or one beat. The *chungmori* movement is also in compound time, though the pulse is marked as a dotted minim rather than a dotted crochet.[11] A change in pulse occurs again in the *chungjungmori* movement, this time from a dotted minim back to a dotted crochet, but at a much faster pace. It is in this movement that Kim Chukp'a begins to add noticeable rubato, manipulating regularity, whereas in the previous movement the pulse was perceptible and constant. This provides a further example of the process of transcoding, whereby the instigation of a fixed code, in this case at the fundamental level of a pulse, is gradually eroded.

The *chajinmori* rhythmic cycle is the most complex cycle of the piece, in that the underlying beat is the most ambiguous of all movements, created through the increased use of hemiola. As a consequence, in Chapter 3, Chaesuk Lee drew attention to the difficulty that performers have in starting the cycle together. The rhythmic interaction of the *kayagŭm* with the cycle undermines the dotted crochet pulse, creating ambiguity; this is enhanced by the accented ninth quaver in the rhythmic cycle which, depending on the rhythmic articulation of the melody, can feel like a downbeat. Using a Deleuzian approach, we can see how rhythm works in the space in-between the evenness and uniform metrical division of time, transcoding such uniform division. Although such time is still located in *Chronos*, the regulated succession of a clear measured beat becomes increasingly uncertain. Notation 5.1 shows the interaction of the beat with the melody performed by the *kayagŭm* at cycles 53–6.[12]

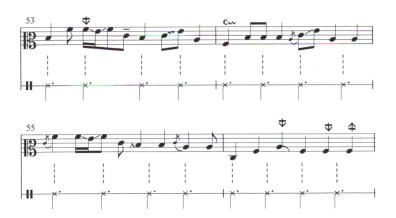

Notation 5.1 The displacement and coincidence of beat in the *chajinmori* cycle

---

[11] Note, though, that the Korean convention is to give *chungmori* as 12/4, indicating each crotchet/eighth beat as the pulse. Since this is adopted universally, we have retained the 12/4 time signature here.

[12] The beat as given here is not performed by the drum player, but is given to show the relationship between the rhythm of melody and pulse.

The *hwimori* movement of Kim Chukp'a's *sanjo* includes some of the most interesting temporal processes. A particularly intriguing melodic and rhythmic example appears near the end of the movement, beginning in cycle 134, where a fast flicking passage combines with a long glissando, the notation of which is slightly incongruous with the aural result. Two distinct periods of time are needed to articulate two definite pitches. However, a glissando is in a sense non-rhythmical in that although a period of time occurs between its start and very end, demarcated divisions of time, which would occur between two definite pitches, are not present. It is articulated through speed – 'the floating line that knows only speeds' seems particularly apt – rather than through rhythm. Although there is a certain rhythmic element given by the movement of the fingers, the music is arguably not metrically defined. At the end of the glissando the music proceeds almost directly to a *senza misura* section, where the zither player performs without conscious reference to a pulse. So, although the drum player repetitively articulates the model rhythmic cycle, this is distinct from the melody.

The same procedure occurs in the *sesanjoshi* movement, though with a further change in pulse, this time from dotted crochet to simple crochet within a 4/4 metre. 4/4 is the simplest metre in the music, and in relation to the metres of the previous movements, the most differentiated. *Sanjo* thus starts and ends with music that is devoid of any conscious reference to a pulse, with the overall rhythmic outline being one of gradual acceleration – a category of speed. The metrical divisions of the rhythmic cycles become more ambiguous, to a point, whereby the music is involved to a fast flicking glissando that releases into a non-pulsed *senza misura*, followed by the most contextually differentiated of metres encountered. If rhythmic cycles are considered to be codes, a process of deterritorialization occurs, with the 'destabilization and ultimately the elimination of established codes that confer fixed meaning'. This rhythmic interaction occurs in the wider context of *Chronos* and *Aeon*, between the plane of organization and the plane of consistency, the latter of which 'is constantly extricating itself' from the former, 'causing particles to spin off the strata, scrambling forms by dint of speed and slowness, breaking down functions' (Deleuze and Guattari 1987: 238–9).

Articulation and Mode

We can now return to mode, and refocus our attention away from the descriptive nature of our analysis in Chapter 4. While rhythmic cycles are often implicit, articulation has a similar relationship to mode: mode acts as a structuring device with which the zither player, through a variety of articulation, transcodes, whereas the drum player transcodes the coded model of a cycle to become expressive. Hence, while musicological descriptions of mode in Korea are abstract representations, it is clear from the 'in-between' nature of some melodies in Kim Chukp'a's *sanjo* that the representations themselves need not be followed exactly or absolutely in performance. Using Deleuzian terminology, mode can be considered as the milieu component, with the player, through articulation acting at the annexed milieu, transcoding this to make it expressive.[13] Due to the highly fluid nature of mode in *kayagŭm sanjo*, the manifestation of which is enabled primarily by the ability of the zither to bend a string to produce a number of distinct pitches or to articulate different degrees of vibrato, mode is never as highly codified as it arguably is in much Western music.[14]

To emphasize the importance of articulation one only has to consider that the raising or falling of a note by bending a particular string can elicit a different mode or modal flavour; this is particularly the case when switching between f and e, played on one string, and correspondingly changing the flavour from *p'yŏngjo* mode to *kyemyŏnjo* mode. In *sanjo* it is articulation, including the use of different kinds of vibrato that act as indicators of different modes, that retains the identity of particular melodies with specific regions or styles, even when the intervallic structure of the mode may mirror another. Hence, with *kyemyŏnjo*, the significance of the vibrating tone and breaking tone. Howard (2002), reflecting his studies on Korean regional folksong and comparing Korean musicological accounts, comments that some scholars have tended to eliminate ornamentation and 'straighten out' errant pitches in their accounts of melody and mode: we argue that it is precisely because of ornamentation and the use of additional pitches that highly fluid modal change and regional identity is made possible. In addition, such articulation allows a process of destabilization to occur, aiming to eliminate established codes (the modes) that confer fixed meaning. Deleuze's observation that transcoding or transduction 'is the manner in which one milieu serves as the basis for another, or conversely is established atop another milieu, dissipates in it or is constituted in it', is appropriate. This makes sense of the statement by Um Hae-kyung that in *p'ansori* (but, we would add, distinct from the processes of Western classical music), some songs have a *kyemyŏnjo* modal structure but use a *p'yŏngjo* singing style (1992: 141). As singing style transcodes mode in *p'ansori*, articulation in *sanjo* shares the same function; good examples of this occur in the *chungjungmori* movement.

Territory and Melody

Interaction between rhythm and rhythmic cycles, and between articulation and mode, are examples of how milieu components can combine, creating expressive assemblages and territories, in the case of *kayagŭm sanjo* through melody. The expressive qualities – that is, musical qualities such as particular inflexions associated with a specific player or region of Korea – acquire temporal constancy in a similar way to how colour, as discussed earlier, can become a territorial marker for tropical fish. The processes that lead to this temporal constancy are never entirely static, because there will always be destabilization of established codes. Indeed, the migrations of *sanjo* musicians from place to place, and the democratization of musical training underway in Korea since the introduction of traditional music teaching in universities, have allowed new relationships and new territories to form.

---

[13]   In our discussion of milieu we suggested that articulation can be seen as an annexed milieu. This is implied here.

[14]   In addition to this, we noted in Chapter 4 that the zither tuning enables a particularly fluid movement between modes.

Through temporal constancy, though, expressive qualities find an objectivity. What is crucial here is that the associations certain melodies have with a specific region or province are constituted by particular modes, articulations and rhythmic cycles. To give an example, and as explored in Chapter 4, in the *chungmori* movement of Kim Chukp'as *kayagŭm sanjo* the second extended melody is reminiscent of the Kangsan school; moving southwards from the capital of Seoul, it is one stage closer to Chŏlla (and to the *kyemyŏnjo* mode), giving considerable and regular vibrato to the dominant, g. The geographical movement in the music, created by the relationships between different melodies derived from different modes, illustrates how, in Deleuze's words, 'expressive qualities or matters of expression enter shifting relations with one another', expressing 'the relation of the territory they draw'. It is this that makes the treatment of melody in *sanjo* particularly intriguing.

The concepts of deterritorialization and involution are particularly useful in developing an understanding of the way that melodic phrases are dispersed through a performance.[15] They allow for a philosophical description of the way in which a differential process occurs whereby particular notes become more prominent than others. As the consideration of the *chinyangjo* movement in Chapter 4 demonstrated, the relationship between phrase and extended melody is extremely complex. Deleuze describes music as the 'active, creative operation which consists of deterritorializing the refrain' (Deleuze and Guattari 1987: 300), with the description of refrain given by Bogue as referring 'to any kind of rhythmic or melodic pattern that stakes out a territory' (2003: 16–17). In *kayagŭm sanjo*, the melodic territory is continually in a process of decoding and, ultimately, does not allow the establishment of codes that confer fixed meaning. Just as Messiaen's translations of birdsong undergo mutation and transformation, so a similar process occurs in *sanjo*.

Transformation or decoding melodic phrases occurs in individual movements as well as across movements. In the former, it occurs at a simpler level due to the continuing relationship to a single metre, while in the latter mutation occurs in rhythmic articulation due to the differing relationships to underlying rhythmic cycles. Recalling that decoding does not refer to 'the process of translating a secret meaning or message into clearer form', but rather to a process of 'dis-investing given meanings altogether' and 'destabilization and ultimately the elimination of established codes', just as a constant repetition of a model rhythmic cycle establishes and fixes the code but is not expressive, so too with melody. The constant and exact repetition of a melody would codify it, but this does not happen with the repetition of melodic phrases in *sanjo*.

The *chinyangjo* movement provides clear examples of transmutation. One only has to look at the initial first four cycles, in *ujo* mode, to see manipulation of the a–e–d motif, together with an a–g–a slide. There is also ambiguity in the pitch e, which due to ornamentation may be raised by almost a semitone. Comparing cycle 4 to cycles 9 and 13 illustrates melodic transformations in each that use increasingly complex articulation – pitch inflexion, string bending and vibrato. Cycles 5 and 14 provide a second example of change through pitch articulation and melodic transformation,

---

[15]   Here, 'melodic phrase' refers to the way that particular phrases contained within an extended melody are transformed.

particularly in beats 3 and 5, although the two cycles share a melodic contour. Cycles 23 and 29, in *kyemyŏnjo* mode, present similar processes of transformation.

The manipulation of a single melodic phrase also occurs across movements. Comparison can be made between the second melodic phrase of the opening *tasŭrŭm* section and cycle 5 of the *chinyangjo* movement, although, of course, the latter is underpinned by a rhythmic cycle. These two *ujo* phrases can be compared with cycle 34 of the *chungmori* movement and cycle 53 of the *chajinmori* movement, where the perception of phrases changes due to the relationship with different rhythmic cycles; indeed, it is rhythmic modification rather than change in articulation that is most important. Further examples of transcoding in a different mode, this time using the Kangsan school, can be found in cycle 39 of the *chinyangjo* movement, in cycle 51 of the *chungmori* movement, and in cycles 13 and 14 of the *chungjungmori* movement.

In the Deleuzian sense, melodies can be considered refrains that are constantly decoded. This is what happens as *sanjo* progresses, occurring at both the micro and macro levels – that is, both within and across movements. Articulation and rhythmic transformation enable decoding, whereby melodic phrases are disinvested of fixed meaning. Particular melodies may have associations with certain regions, but in *sanjo* the constituents of these same melodic phrases is not unchanging, nor fixed, but extremely fluid. So, melodic phrases are analogical to the open equation $+ y + z + a$, rather than the closed $x = x = $ not y.

At the end of our discussion of Deleuzian philosophy above, we drew attention to the notion of involution, suggesting that the term does not refer to a process of regression but to one of increased differentiation. In a similar way to how metre becomes more differentiated – that is, as there is a gradual change from more complex compound metres to a simpler duple metre as the performance of *sanjo* progresses – so it is with pitch. One tone in particular, c, which is the tonic in *kyemyŏnjo* mode, is fundamental to *sanjo*, not least due to its placement as the middle string of the zither itself,[16] and it is through the process of involution that this pitch becomes the most differentiated. Put simply, the pitch content of melodic phrases reduces as *sanjo* progresses, gradually centring more and more around the tone c. Comparison of melodic phrases from all the movements of Kim Chukp'a's *sanjo* shows an overall predominance of this note, and it is this note that is the least articulated, in the sense that it is rarely accorded vibrato, pitch inflexion or string bending. In particular, the *hwimori* and *sesanjoshi* movements late in the performance show the highest occurrence of c, which can be coupled to the dominant, g, to give the total tonal palette for a melodic phrase.

One last point should be made about glissando in the *hwimori* movement. Noted earlier as important in regards to rhythmic articulation, it is also significant in its use of pitch. Distinct pitches are not defined in a true glissando, though c in the case of Kim Chukp'a's *sanjo* is still given differentiation and a certain prominence. Within *hwimori*, melody is combined with rhythm, existing in the intersect between *Chronos* and the floating line of *Aeon*. At this point, mode, due to the lack of defined pitch, is at its most highly decoded and, indeed, it could be argued that it does not exist at all.

---

[16]   And, in this, the term milieu seems all the more poignant.

Concluding Remarks

The complexity of Deleuze's philosophy arises, not least, because of the way defined concepts are in a constant state of flux. Such concepts are not reducible to a singular identity but, rather, are contextual, allowing for the explication of multiple relationships, which in our discussion of Kim Chukp'a's *sanjo* have ranged from the interaction that performers have with their instruments and with each other to the intricate temporal relationship between *Chronos* and *Aeon*. In this chapter, we have used concepts to provide both a philosophical framework and also to elucidate musical processes contained within the music. Organizational principles are apparent, and different modes, rhythmic cycles and articulation all act as such. However, other principles are also at work, used to undermine any codification process at both the rhythmic and melodic level.

In this chapter, then, we have sought to move forward from a reliance on mode as the primary organizational feature of *sanjo*, and in so doing we have attempted to open up a discourse that can match Korean musicological to Western philosophical perspectives. To do so is needed because our understanding requires building flexibility into musical grammar, and into the rules that govern structure and form. The reason is because the music of *sanjo* constantly extricates itself from absolute organizational principles. Examples of how this happens can be found in the interaction of rhythms with rhythmic cycles and the transcoding and ultimately decoding of melody with the differentiation of particular notes. It is through processes such as these that *sanjo* associates itself with different principles of organization than those used in much Western music, aligning itself more in the plane of consistency. This sets *sanjo* apart, demonstrating its quality, vibrancy, and significance not just on a Korean but on a global stage.

Chapter 6

Kim Chukp'a's *Sanjo*: Notation

Tasŭrŭm

Chinyangjo

[2: *Ujo (Kyemyŏnsŏng)*]

[3: *Ujo* (*Kyemyŏnsŏng*)]

[7: *Kyemyŏnjo* (*Pyŏnch'ŏng*)]

[9: *Kyemyŏnjo*]

[11: *Kyemyŏnjo*]

Chungmori

[1: *Kyŏngdŭrŭm (Kyŏngjo)*]

[2: *Kangsanje*]

Chungjungmori

[1: *Kangsanje*]

[*Pyŏngjo Kangsanje*]

Chajinmori

[3: *Ujo*]

[5: *Kyemyŏnjo*]

Hwimori

[1: *Kyemyŏnjo*]

Sesanjoshi

[1: *Kyemyŏnjo*]

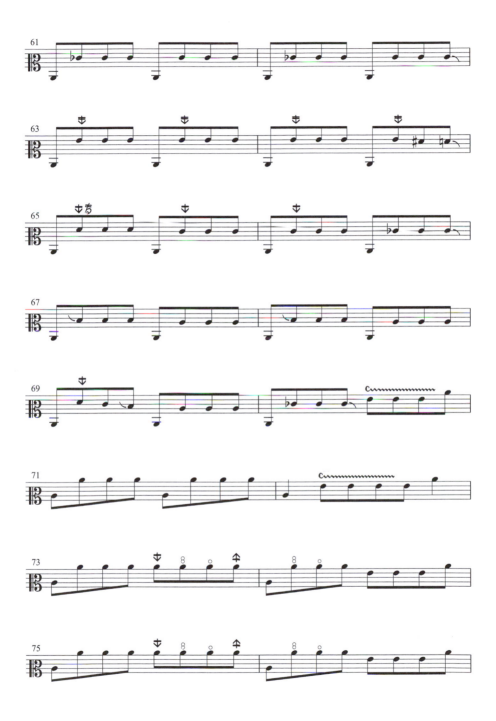

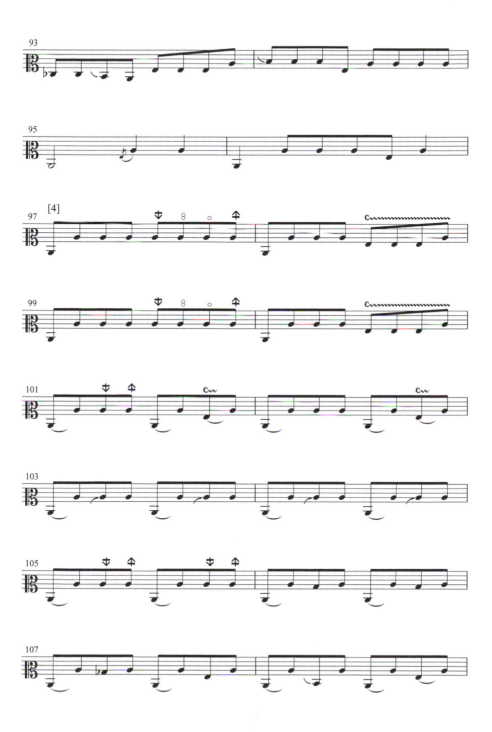

[5: *Pyŏnch'ŏng Kangsanje*]

[Kangsanje]

[*Mujangdan*]
sensa misura

References

Adriaansz, Willem, *The Kumiuta and Danmono Traditions of Japanese Koto Music* (Berkeley and Los Angeles: University of California Press, 1973).

Appadurai, Arjun, *Modernity at Large: Cultural Dimensions of Globalization* (Minneapolis: University of Minnesota Press, 1996).

Bogue, Ronald, *Deleuze on Music, Painting, and the Arts* (New York and London: Routledge, 2003).

Bogue, Ronald, *Deleuze's Wake: Tributes and Tributaries* (New York: State of New York Press, 2004).

Boulez, Pierre, *Boulez on Music Today*, trans. Susan Bradshaw and Richard Rodney Bennett (Cambridge, MA: Harvard University Press, 1971).

Buchanan, Ian and Marcel Swiboda, eds, *Deleuze and Music* (Edinburgh: Edinburgh University Press, 2004).

Chang Sahun, *Han'guk akki taegwan* (Seoul: Han'guk kugak hakhoe, 1969).

Chang Sahun, *Kugak ch'ongnon* (Seoul: Chŏngŭmsa, 1976).

Chang Sahun, *Kugaksaron* (Seoul: Susŏwŏn, 1983).

Chang Sahun, *Kugak taesajŏn* (Seoul: Segwang ŭmak ch'ulp'ansa, 1984).

Chang Sahun, *Han'guk ŭmakkwa muyonge kwanhan yŏn'gu* (Seoul: Segwang ŭmak ch'ulp'ansa, 1993).

Chang Sahun and Han Manyŏng, *Kugak kaeron* (Seoul: Han'guk kugak hakhoe, 1975).

Cho Wimin, *Hyŏn'gŭm sanjobo* (unpublished, 1967).

Cho Wimin, 'Hyŏn'gŭm sanjo ŭi wŏnhyŏnggwa hyŏnhaenghyŏng', *Yi Hyegu paksa songsu kinyŏm: ŭmakhak nonch'ong/Essays in Korean Music*: 221–65 (Seoul: Han'guk kugak hakhoe, 1969).

Ch'oe Ch'unshik, *Han'guginege munhwanŭn innŭn'ga?* (Seoul: Sagyejul, 1997).

Ch'oe Ch'unshik, *Han'guginege munhwaga ŏptago?* (Seoul: Sagyejul, 2000).

Ch'oe T'aehyŏn, *Haegŭm sanjo yŏn'gu* (Seoul: Segwang ŭmak ch'ulp'ansa, 1988).

Chŏn Inp'yŏng, *Han'guk chakkok inmun/A Guide in Musical Composition for Korean Instruments* (Seoul: Hyŏndae ŭmak ch'ulp'ansa, 1989).

Chŏng Noshik, *Chosŏn ch'anggŭksa* (Seoul: Chosŏn ilbosa, 1940).

Chŏng Pŏmt'ae, *Myŏngin myŏngch'ang* (Seoul: Kip'ŭnsaem, 2002).

Chŏng Pyŏnguk, *Han'guk ŭi p'ansori* (Seoul: Chimmundang, 1981).

Chu Yŏngwi, 'Hyŏn'gŭm sanjo ŭi cho-e taehan yŏn'gu', in *Chŏnt'ong yesulwŏn*, eds, *Sanjo ŭi ŭmakhakchŏk yŏn'gu*: 367–408 (Seoul: Minsogwŏn, 2004).

Crossley-Holland, Peter C., 'Chinese Music', in Eric Blom, ed., *The Grove Dictionary of Music and Musicians* 2: 219–48 (London: Macmillan, 1959).

Deleuze, Gilles and Félix Guattari, *Anti-Oedipus: Capitalism and Schizophrenia*, trans. Robert Hurley, Mark Seem and Helen R. Lane (Minneapolis: University of Minnesota, 1977).

Deleuze, Gilles and Félix Guattari, *A Thousand Plateaus: Capitalism and Schizophrenia*, trans. Brian Massumi (Minneapolis: University of Minnesota Press, 1987).

Diamond, Jody, 'There is no they there', *ETHNOForum* (Baltimore: University of Maryland, Baltimore College, 1990).

Dorchieva, E. N., *Metodika orujeniya igre na yatage* (Ulan Ude: Informalis, 2006).

Dournon, Geneviève, 'Organology', in Helen Myers, ed., *Ethnomusicology: An Introduction*. New Grove Handbooks in Musicology: 245–300 (London: Macmillan, 1992).

Feld, Steven, *Sound and Sentiment* (Philadelphia: University of Pennsylvania Press, 1982).

Feld, Steven, 'pygmy POP: a genealogy of schizophonic mimesis', *Yearbook for Traditional Music* 28 (1996): 1–35.

Flavin, Philip, '*Ryuha*: the construction of tradition in Japanese music', unpublished paper presented at the conference of the Society for Ethnomusicology, Miami (2003).

Gulik, Robert H. van, 'Brief note on the *cheng*, the Chinese cither', *Toyo Ongaku Kenkyu* 9 (1951).

Hahn Man-young [Han Manyŏng], 'Folksong', in *Survey of Korean Traditional Arts: Folk Arts*: 306–18 (Seoul: National Academy of Arts, 1974).

Hahn Man-young, *Kugak: Studies in Korean Traditional Music* (Seoul: Tamgu Dang, 1990).

Ham Hwajin, *Chosŏn ŭmak t'ongnon* (Seoul: Ŭryu munhwasa, 1948).

Ham Tongjŏngwŏl, *Murŭn kŏnyŏ pwaya algo, saramŭn kyŏkkŏ pwaya algŏdŭn/The Deep-Rooted Tree Oral Histories 15: The Life of the Kayagŭm Virtuoso Ham Tong-jŏng-wŏl*, transc. and ed. Kim Myŏnggon and Kim Haesuk (Seoul: Ppuri kip'ŭn namu, 1990).

Han Manyŏng, '*P'ansori ŭi ujo*', *Han'guk ŭmak yŏn'gu* 2 (1972): 67–88.

Han Manyŏng, '*Taebaeksanmaegidong chibang ŭi sŏnbŏp ŭi yŏn'gu*', *Yesul nonmunjip* 12 (1973): 121–47.

Han Myŏnghŭi, '*Hyŏndae kugak*', in Yi Haerang, ed., *Han'guk ŭmaksa*: 409–76 (Seoul: Taehan min'guk yesulwŏn, 1985).

Han Pŏmsu, *Taegŭm sanjobo* (Seoul: Minhaksa, 1975).

Holland, Eugene W., *Deleuze and Guattari's Anti-Oedipus: Introduction to Schizoanalysis* (New York: Routledge, 1999).

Howard, John Tasked and James Lyons, *Modern Music: A Popular Guide to Greater Musical Enjoyment* (New York: Mentor, 1957. Originally published, 1942, by Thomas Y. Crowell Company).

Howard, Keith, 'The Deep-Rooted Tree *P'ansori* collection', *Korea Journal* 23/11 (1983): 58–65.

Howard, Keith, *Korean Musical Instruments: A Practical Guide* (Seoul: Se-kwang Music Publishers, 1988).

Howard, Keith, *Bands, Songs, and Shamanistic Rituals: Folk Music in Korean Society* (Seoul: Korea Branch of the Royal Asiatic Society, 1989; second edition, 1990).

Howard, Keith, 'The Korean *kayagŭm*: the making of a zither', *Papers of the British Association for Korean Studies* 5 (1994): 1–22.

Howard, Keith, 'Performers, teachers, and scholars. Notation systems for Korean melody and rhythm', *Han'guk ŭmaksa hangnon* XX (1998): 593–629.

Howard, Keith, 'Mode as a scholarly construct in Korean music', *The Ratio Book*: 176–97. *Feedback Papers 43* (Köln: Feedback Studio Verlag, 2001).

Howard, Keith, 'Lee Hye-Ku and the Development of Korean Musicology', *Acta Koreana*, 5/1 (January 2002): 77–99.

Howard, Keith, 'Seoul Blues: the determinants of emotion in Korean music', in Michel Demeuldre, ed., *Sentiments doux-amers dans les musiques du monde: Délectations moroses dans les blues, fado, tango, flamenco, rebetiko, p'ansori, ghazal...*: 155–67 (Brussels: L'Harmattan, 2004).

Howard, Keith, *Preserving Korean Music: Intangible Cultural Properties as Icons of Identity* (Aldershot: Ashgate, 2006).

Howard, Keith, *Creating Korean Music: Tradition, Innovation and the Discourse of Identity* (Aldershot: Ashgate, 2006).

Hwang Chunyŏn, '*Akhak kwebŏm ŭi hyangakcho*', *Han'guk ŭmaksa hangnon* 11 (1993): 425–40.

Hwang Jun-yon [Hwang Chunyŏn], 'On changing our name', *Tongyang ŭmak/ Journal of the Asian Music Research Institute)* 20 (1998): v.

Hwang Pyŏnggi, *Chŏng Nam-hŭi and Hwang Byungki Sanjo School (Tchalbŭn kayagŭm sanjo moŭm, Chŏng Namhŭi-je Hwang Pyŏnggi ryu)* (Seoul: Ihwa yŏja taehakkyo ch'ulp'anbu, 1998).

Hwang Pyŏnggi, '*Yŏngam-gun sanjo haksul taehoe ŭi yŏksajŏk ŭiŭi*', in *Kayagŭm sanjo hyŏnjang saŏp ch'ujin wiwŏnhoe, eds, Sanjo yŏn'gu. Sanjo ch'angshija aksa Kim Ch'angjo kinyŏm nonmun t'ŭkchip* 1: 35–7 (Seoul: Ŭnha ch'ulp'ansa, 2001).

Hwang Pyŏngju, '*Kayagŭm ŭi kaeryange kwanhan yŏn'gu: 17-chul kayagŭmŭl chungshimŭro*', in *Kugak nonmunjip* 2: 33–55 (Seoul: Kungnip kugagwŏn, 1990).

Jairazhboy, Nazir Ali, 'An explication of the Sachs-Hornbostel instrument classification system', in *Selected Reports in Ethnomusicology 8: Issues in Organology*: 81–104 (Los Angeles: Department of Ethnomusicology and Systematic Musicology, UCLA, 1990).

Johnson, Henry, *The Koto: A Traditional Instrument in Contemporary Japan* (Tokyo: Hotei Publishing, 2004).

Kang Hanyŏng, *Shin Chaehyo p'ansori sasŏl chip* (Seoul: Posŏng munhwasa, 1977).

Kaufmann, Walter, *Musical References in the Chinese Classics*. Detroit Monographs in Musicology 5 (Detroit: Information Co-ordinators, 1976).

Kayagŭm sanjo hyŏnjang saŏp ch'ujin wiwŏnhoe, eds, *Sanjo yŏn'gu. Sanjo ch'angshija aksa Kim Ch'angjo kinyŏm nonmun t'ŭkchip* 1 (Seoul: Ŭnha ch'ulp'ansa, 2001).

Keil, Charles and Steven Feld, *Music Grooves* (Chicago: Chicago University Press, 1994).

Kenzō, Hayashi, *Shōsōin gakki no kenkyū* (Tokyo: Kazama shobō, 1964).

Kenzō, Hayashi, '*Shillagŭm (kayagŭm) ŭi saengsŏng*', trans. Hwang Chunyŏn, *Minjok ŭmakhak* 6 (1984): 135–40.

Kim Chŏngja, '*Kayagŭm sanjo ŭi ujowa kyemyŏnjo: chinyangjo-e wihayŏ*', in *Yi Hyegu paksa songsu kinyŏm: ŭmakhak nonch'ong/Essays in Korean Music*: 1–33 (Seoul: Han'guk kugak hakhoe, 1969).

Kim Chŏngja, '*Kungnip kugagwŏn ŭi yŏngsan hoesanggwa minjok chul p'ungnyu ŭi pigyo yŏn'gu*', in *Tongyang ŭmak nonch'ong/Articles on Asian Music: Festschrift for Dr Chang Sa-hun*: 37–64 (Seoul: Han'guk kugak hakhoe, 1977).

Kim Haesuk, *Sanjo yŏn'gu* (Seoul: Segwang ŭmak ch'ulp'ansa, 1987).

Kim, Hee-sun, 'The development of a *sanjo* school: a case study of the Kim Yun-duk kayagum sanjo' (unpublished paper, 2000).

Kim Injae, *Kayagŭm sanjo* (Seoul: Ŭnha ch'ulp'ansa, 1990).

Kim Taesŏk, *Kŏmun'go sanjo* (Seoul: Kwanil munhwasa, 1984).

Kim Tonguk, *Kaya munhak* (Seoul: Ch'ŏnggu taehakkyo, 1966).

Kim Ujin, '*Akki hyŏngt'ae pyŏnhwa-e taehan yŏn'gu: chinyŏn ŭigwe ŭi akkidorŭl chungshimŭro*', *Han'guk ŭmak yŏn'gu* 17/18 (1989): 79–107.

Kishibe, Shigeo, *The Traditional Music of Japan* (Tokyo: The Japan Foundation, 1982).

Kugakki kaeryang wiwŏnhoe, eds, *Kugakki kaeryang chonghap pogosŏ* (Seoul: Kugakki kaeryang wiwŏnhoe, 1998).

Kungnip kugagwŏn, *Han'guk ŭmakhak ch'ongsŏ charyo* 16 (Seoul: Kungnip kugagwŏn, 1984).

Kweon, Sug-In, 'Popular discourses on Korean culture: from the late 1980s to the present', *Korea Journal* 43/1 (2003): 32–57.

Kwŏn Osŏng, '*Samguk shidae ijŏn ŭi aksok*' and '*Samguk shidae ŭi ŭmak*', in Yi Haerang, ed., *Han'guk ŭmaksa*: 9–100 (Seoul: Taehan min'guk yesulwŏn, 1985).

Kwŏn Tohŭi, '*Kayagŭm sanjo chinyang ŭi hyŏngshingnon*', *Han'guk ŭmbanhak* 3 (1993): 89–153.

Kwŏn Tohŭi, '*Kim Ch'angjo sanjo ŭi yangshiksajŏk chomang*', in Kayagŭm sanjo hyŏnjang saŏp ch'ujin wiwŏnhoe, eds, *Sanjo yŏn'gu. Sanjo ch'angshija aksa Kim Ch'angjo kinyŏm nonmun t'ŭkchip* 1: 144–69 (Seoul: Ŭnha ch'ulp'ansa, 2001).

Lee, Byong Won, *Styles and Esthetics in Korean Traditional Music* (Seoul: National Center for Korean Traditional Performing Arts, 1997).

Lee, Byong Won, 'The ornaments in traditional Korean music: structure, function and semantics', *Ssi-ol Almanach 1998/99*: 59–66 (Berlin: Internationale Isang Yun Gesellschaft e.V, 1999).

Lee, Byong Won, 'Western staff notation and its impact on Korean musical practice', in *In Search of New Creativity: The Changing Values of Music*: 79–90 (Seoul: Asian Music Research Institute, Seoul National University, 2000).

Lee, Chaesuk [Yi Chaesuk], '*Kayagŭm sanjo chung chajinmori rhythm hyŏngt'ae yŏn'gu*/A study of *chajinmori* rhythms of *kayagŭm sanjo*', *Ŭmak hakpo* 4 (Seoul: Seoul National University, 1967).

Lee, Chaesuk, '*Kayagŭm sanjo ŭi t'ŭre kwanhan sogo*/A study of the patterns in *kayagŭm sanjo*', *Yi Hyegu paksa songsu kinyŏm: ŭmakhak nonch'ong/Essays in Korean Music*: 135–51 (Seoul: Han'guk kugak hakhoe, 1969).

Lee, Chaesuk, *Kayagŭm sanjo* (Seoul: Unha ch'ulp'ansa, 1971).

Lee, Chaesuk, '*Yanggŭm chubŏbe kwanhan sogo*', *Han'guk ŭmak yŏn'gu/Journal of the Korean Musicological Society* 2 (1972): 45–66.

Lee, Chaesuk, '*Sanjo*', in *Survey of Korean Arts: Traditional Music*: 202–11 (Seoul: National Academy of Arts, 1973).

Lee, Chaesuk, '*Ch'oe Oksam ryu kayagŭm sanjogo/Kayagŭm sanjo* of the Ch'oe Oksam school', *Chang Sahun paksa hoegap kinyŏm tongyang ŭmakhak nonch'ong/Articles on Asian Music, Festschrift for Dr. Chang Sa-hun*: 115–34 (Seoul: Han'guk ŭmak hakhoe/Korean Musicological Society, 1977).

Lee, Chaesuk, *Kugak panjubŏp/Rhythm in the Court Music and Sanjo* (Seoul: Sumundang, 1979).

Lee, Chaesuk, *Kayagŭm sanjo, Ch'oe Oksam ryu/Kayagum Sanjo of Ch'oe, Ok-sam School with Changgo accompaniment* (Seoul: Sumundang, 1981).

Lee, Chaesuk, *Kayagŭm sanjo, Kim Chukp'a ryu/Kayagum Sanjo of Kim, Chuk-Pa School with Changgo accompaniment* (Seoul: Susŏwŏn, 1983).

Lee, Chaesuk, '*Kŭnse kayagŭm yŏnjubŏp ŭi pyŏnch'ŏn*/Transition of *kayagŭm* technique since the 18th century', *Minjok ŭmak 6/Journal of the Asian Music Research Institute* 6 (1984): 17–30.

Lee, Chaesuk, *Kayagŭm sanjo, Sŏng Kumyŏn ryu/Kayagum Sanjo of Sŏng, Kŭm-Yŏn School with Changgo accompaniment* (Seoul: Segwang ŭmak ch'ulp'ansa, 1987).

Lee, Chaesuk, *Kayagŭm sanjo, Kang T'aehong ryu* (Seoul: Unha ch'ulp'ansa, 1996).

Lee, Chaesuk, ed., *Chosŏnjo kungjung ŭirye wa ŭmak/Court Rituals and Music of the Chosŏn Dynasty* (Seoul: Sŏul tehakkyo ch'ulp'anbu, 1998).

Lee, Chaesuk, '*Kayagŭm ŭi kujo wa chubŏp ŭi pyŏnch'ŏn*/The development of the construction and performance techniques of the kayagŭm', *Yi Hyegu paksa kusun kinyŏm ŭmakhak nonch'ong/Essays in Musicology, An Offering in Celebration of Lee Hye-ku on his Ninetieth Birthday*: 345–76 (Seoul: Seoul National University, 1998).

Lee, Chaesuk, 'The development of the construction and performance techniques of the *kayagŭm*', in Nathan Hesselink, ed., *Contemporary Directions: Korean Folk Music Engaging the Twentieth Century and Beyond*: 96–120. Korean Research Monograph 27 (Berkeley: Center for Korean Studies, University of California, Berkeley, 2001).

Lee Hye-Ku [Yi Hyegu], 'Introduction to Korean music', *Korea Journal* 16/12 (1976): 4–14.

Lee Hye-Ku, 'Quintuple meter in Korean traditional music', *Asian Music* 13/1 (1981a): 19–29.

Lee Hye-Ku, *Yŏngsan Hoesang: Mass in the Spiritual Mountain* (programme notes for 4-LP set). Seoul: Sung Eum (SEL-100 122), 1981b.

Lee Hye-Ku, *Essays on Korean Traditional Music*, trans. Robert C. Provine (Seoul: Korea Branch of the Royal Asiatic Society, 1981c).

Lee, Jae-kyung, *Korean Gayageum: A Playing Guide* (Seoul: Minsogwŏn, 2003).

Lee Sŏng-ch'ŏn [Yi Sŏngch'ŏn], '*Samhyŏn yukkak* ("wind ensemble")', *Survey of Korean Arts: Traditional Music*: 128–35 (Seoul: National Academy of Arts, 1973).

Lee Sŏngmu, 'The rise of *chungin* and their characteristics', *Papers of the British Association for Korean Studies* 1 (1991): 107–16.

Liang, Ming Yueh, '*Zheng*', in Stanley Sadie, ed., *The New Grove Dictionary of Musical Instruments* 3: 893–4 (London: Macmillan, 1984).

Lim, Susie, 'Finding the "flow": the *ryu* canon and new *ryu*', unpublished paper presented at the conference of the Society for Ethnomusicology, Miami (2003).

Lomax, Alan, 'Appeal for cultural equity', in Thomas Vennum Jr, ed., *1985 Festival of American Folklife:* 40–46 (Washington: Smithsonian Institution, 1985).

Messiaen, Olivier, *Technique de mon langage musical* (Paris: Alphonse Leduc, 1944). English trans., *The Technique of my Musical Language* (Paris: Alphonse Leduc, 1956).

Mun Chaesuk, *Chukp'a. Kayagŭm kokchip* (Seoul: Segwang ŭmak ch'ulp'ansa, 1989).

Mun Chaesuk, *Kim Chukp'a kayagŭm sanjo yŏn'gu* (Seoul: Hyŏndae ŭmak ch'ulp'ansa, 2000).

Mun Chaesuk, *Yŏngsan hoesang. Iwan'kyu Kim Chukp'a sojang akpo ch'ungsŏ 1* (Seoul: Minsogwŏn, 2001).

Mun Hyŏn, *Kaeryang kugakkijŏn. Kungnip kugagwŏn yeaktang kaegwan kinyŏm* (Seoul: Kungnip kugagwŏn, 1996).

Munhwa kongbobu, *Chungyo muhyŏng munwajae haesŏl: ŭmak p'yŏn* (Seoul: Munhwajae kwalliguk/Munhwa kongbobu, 1985).

Nixon, Andrea, '*Yatga*' and '*Yatagulig*', in Stanley Sadie, ed., *The New Grove Dictionary of Musical Instruments* 3: 884 (London: Macmillan, 1984).

Paek, Inok, 'Music for the fatherland: the North Korean soundscape in the construction of Chongryun identity in Japan', *Papers of the British Association for Korean Studies* 10 (2005): 135–45.

Paek Taeung, '*P'ansori-e issŏsŏ ŭi ujo, p'yŏngjo, kyemyŏnjo*', *Han'guk ŭmak yŏn'gu* 8/9 (1979): 149–203.

Paek Taeung, '*Insok ŭmak ŭi sŏnbŏpchŏk yangsang: kkŏngnŭnmoge taehayŏ*', MA dissertation (Seoul: Seoul National University, 1981).

Paek Taeung, *Han'guk chŏnt'ong ŭmak ŭi sŏnyul kujo* (Seoul: Tamgwang ch'ulp'ansa, 1982).

Pak Hŏnbong, *Chŏngak taegang* (Seoul: Kugak yesul hakkyo ch'ulp'anbu, 1966).

Pak Hŏnbong, *Kayagŭm sanjo. Muhyŏng munhwajae chosa pogosŏ* 39 (Seoul: Munhwajae kwalliguk, 1967).

Pak Hyŏngsŏp, *Chosŏn minjok akki* (Pyongyang: Munye ch'ulp'ansa, 1994).

Pak Pŏmhun, *P'iri sanjo yŏn'gu* (Seoul: Segwang ŭmak ch'ulp'ansa, 1985).

Pak Pŏmhun, *Chakkok p'yŏn'gogŭl wihan kugakki ihae* (Seoul: Segwang ŭmak ch'ulp'ansa, 1991).

Park, Chan E., *Voices from the Straw Mat: Toward an Ethnography of Korean Story Singing. Hawai'i Studies on Korea* (Honolulu: University of Hawai'i Press, 2003).

Piston, Walter, *Orchestration* (London: Gollancz, 1955/1969).

Potter, Keith, *Four Musical Minimalists: La Monte Young, Terry Riley, Steve Reich, Philip Glass* (Cambridge: Cambridge University Press, 2002).

Pratt, Keith, *Korean Music. Its History and Its Performance* (Seoul: Jung Eum Sa and London: Faber Music, 1987).

Rice, Timothy, 'Time, place, and metaphor in musical experience and ethnography', *Ethnomusicology* 47/2 (2003): 151–79.

Rockwell, Coralie, '*Kayago*: the origin and development of the Korean twelve string zither', *Transactions of the Korea Branch of the Royal Asiatic Society* 49 (1974): 26–47.

Roseman, Marina, *Healing Sounds from the Malaysian Rainforest: Temiar music and medicine* (Berkeley: University of California Press, 1991).

Ryang, Sonia, *North Koreans in Japan: Language, ideology, and identity* (Boulder, CO: Westview, 1997).

Ryang, Sonia, ed., *Koreans in Japan: Critical voices from the margin* (New York: Routledge, 2000).

Schiff, David, *The Music of Elliott Carter* (London: Ernst Eulenberg, 1983).

Song Bang-song [Song Pangsong], *The Sanjo Tradition of Korean Kŏmun'go Music* (Seoul: Jung Eum Sa, 1986).

Song Bang-song, 'Koguryo instruments in Tomb No. 1 at ch'ang-ch'uan, Manchuria, *Musica Asiatica* 6 (1991): 1–17.

Song Bang-song, *Korean Music: Historical and Other Aspects* (Seoul: Jimoondang, 2000).

Song Hyejin, Kim Sŏngjin, Yi Chihyŏn, Pak Hyeyun and Ch'ŏn Kyŏngwŏn, *Kayagŭmŭl wihan ch'angŭijŏk kyosubŏp* (Seoul: Minsogwŏn, 2005).

Song Kwŏnjun, '*Han Pŏmsu haegŭm sanjo ŭi sŏnyul kusŏnge taehan yŏn'gu*', MA dissertation (Seoul: Seoul National University, 1984).

Song Pangsong, *Han'guk ŭmak t'ongsa* (Seoul: Ilchogak, 1984).

Sŏng Shimon, *Kayagŭm chubŏpkwa shilsŭp* (Seoul: Segwang ŭmak ch'ulp'ansa, 1987).

Stivale, Charles J., ed., *Gilles Deleuze: Key Concepts* (Montreal: McGill-Queen's University Press, 2005).

Tran Van Khe, *Vietnam* (Paris: Buchet/Chastel, 1967).

Um Hae-Kyung, *Making P'ansori: Korean Musical Drama*, PhD dissertation (Belfast: Queen's University of Belfast, 1992).

Widdess, D. Richard, 'Involving the performers in transcription and analysis: a collaborative approach to dhrupad', *Ethnomusicology* 38/1 (1994): 59–80.

Willoughby, Heather A., 'The sound of *han*: *P'ansori*, timbre and a Korean ethos of pain and suffering', *Yearbook for Traditional Music* 32 (2000): 17–30.

Willoughby, Heather A., 'Retake: a decade of learning from the movie *Sŏp'yŏnje*', *Ŭmakkwa munhwa/Music and Culture* 8 (2003): 119–43.

Yang Sŭnghŭi, '*Kim Ch'angjo-e kwanhan nambukhan charyo mit munhŏnkoch'are ŭihan kojŭng*', in Kayagŭm sanjo hyŏnjang saŏp ch'ujin wiwŏnhoe, eds, *Sanjo yŏn'gu. Sanjo ch'angshija aksa Kim Ch'angjo kinyŏm nonmun t'ŭkchip* 1: 54–143 (Seoul: Ŭnha ch'ulp'ansa, 2001).

Yi Chaesuk kyosu hoegap kinyŏm haengsach'ujin wiwŏnhoe, eds, *Maehwa hyanggiro p'iŏnanŭn yŏltu norae/Collection of the New Composition for Kayagum: An Offering in Celebration of Lee Chae-Suk's Sixtieth Birthday* (Seoul: Yi Chaesuk kyosu hoegap kinyŏm haengsach'ujin wiwŏnhoe, 2001).

Yi Chinwŏn, '*Yudongch'o t'ungso sanjo ŭi sŏnyul punsŏk*', in Chŏnt'ong yesulwŏn, eds, *Sanjo ŭi ŭmakhakchŏk yŏn'gu*: 253–80 (Seoul: Minsogwŏn, 2004).

Yi Chinwŏn, *Taegŭm sanjo ch'angshija Pak Chonggi p'yŏngjŏn* (Seoul: Minsogwŏn, 2007).

Yi Chiyŏng, '*Kayagŭm sanjo chungjungmori akchang ŭi chogusŏng: Chŏng Namhŭi ŭi sanjorŭl chungshimŭro*', MA dissertation (Seoul: Seoul National University, 1993).

Yi Hyegu, *Han'guk ŭmak yŏn'gu* (Seoul: Kungmin ŭmak yŏn'guhoe, 1957).

Yi Hyegu, *Han'guk ŭmak nonch'ong* (Seoul: Sumundang, 1976).

Yi Hyegu, ed. with commentary, *Akhak kwebŏm. Kojŏn kugyŏk ch'ongsŏ* 199–200 (Seoul: Minjok munhwa ch'ujinhoe, 1979).

Yi Kukcha, '*P'ansori maek ttara 8: Chunggoje myŏngch'ang Pak Tongjin*', *Yehyang* 43 (1988): 204–11.

Yi Kukcha, *P'ansori yesul mihak* (Seoul: Nanam, 1989).

Yi Kyut'ae, *Han'gugin ŭi ŭishik kujo* (Seoul: Shinwŏn ch'ulp'ansa, 1983).

Yi Pohyŏng, '*Mugawa p'ansoriwa sanjoesŏ ŭi ŏnmori karak pigyo*/Melodic patterns of *otmori* music used in shamanistic song, *pan-sori* (dramatic song) and *sanjo* (instrumental music)', in *Yi Hyegu paksa songsu kinyŏm: ŭmakhak nonch'ong/Essays in Korean Music, a Birthday Offering for Lee Hye-Ku*: 81–116 (Seoul: Han'guk kugak hakhoe, 1969).

Yi Pohyŏng, '*Shinawigwŏn ŭi musok ŭmak*', *Han'guk munhwa illyuhak* 4 (1971): 79–96.

Yi Pohyŏng, *Kayagŭm sanjo. Muhyŏng munhwajae chosa pogosŏ* 94 (Seoul: Munhwajae kwalliguk, 1972).

Yi Pohyŏng, '*P'ansori*', *Survey of Korean Arts: Traditional Music*: 212–28 (Seoul: National Academy of Arts, 1973).

Yi Pohyŏng, '*Kayagŭm sanjo*', *Muhyŏng munhwajae (ŭmak) chosa pogosŏ* 2 (Seoul: Munhwajae kwalliguk, 1980).

Yi Pohyŏng, '*Han'guk muŭishik ŭmak*', in *Minjok munhwa yŏn'gu ch'ongsŏ* 6, *Han'guk musok ŭi chonghapchok koch'al*: 209–30 (Seoul: Koryŏ taehakkyo, 1982).

Yi Pohyŏng, '*Kim Ch'angjo ŭi kayagŭm sanjowa hugi (kŭndae) sanjo chŏnsŭngnon*', in *Kayagŭm sanjo hyŏnjang saŏp ch'ujin wiwŏnhoe*, eds, *Sanjo yŏn'gu. Sanjo ch'angshija aksa Kim Ch'angjo kinyŏm nonmun t'ŭkchip* 1: 41–53 (Seoul: Ŭnha ch'ulp'ansa, 2001).

Yoo Byung Eun, 'An interaction and a reaction: aspects of *Piano Sanjo No.2* of Yoo/*Sangho chagyonggwa panjagyong: p'iano sanjo che 2-bŏn ŭi kyŏngu*', in *In Search of New Creativity: The Changing Values of Music*: 171–82. *Proceedings of the International Symposium, the Fifth International Asian Music Conference* (Seoul: Asian Music Research Institute, Seoul National University, 2000).

Yu Hongjun, *Na ŭi munhwa yusan tapsagi* I–III (Seoul: Ch'angbi ch'ulp'ansa, 1993–1997).

Yu Kiryong, '*P'ansori yongŏ* 1–11', *Wŏlgan munhwajae* 95 (1979): 23–6, 96 (1980a): 32–5, 97 (1980b): 19–22, 98 (1980c): 24–6, 100 (1980d): 28–30, 103 (1980e): 35–7, 104 (1980f): 15–17, 105 (1980g): 18–20, 107 (1981a): 9–11, 108 (1981b): 38–40, 109 (1981c): 32–4.

Yu Kiryong and Hong Yunshik, *Kyŏnggi shinawi. Muhyŏng munhwajae chosa pogosŏ* 54 (Seoul: Munhwajae kwalliguk, 1968).

Yu, Siu Wah, 'Constructing *liupai* (schools) of Chinese solo instrumental music', unpublished paper presented at the conference of the Society for Ethnomusicology, Miami (2003).

Yun Chunggang and Chŏng Hyŏn'gyŏng, *Kŭriun Sŏng Kŭmyŏn* (Seoul: Minsogwŏn, 2003).

Zemp, Hugo, *Musique dan: La musique et la pensée et la vie sociale d'une société africaine* (Paris: Mouton, 1981).

Discography

Selected Recordings by Chaesuk Lee

Pada. Yi Sŏngch'ŏn kayagŭm chakp'umjip (Shinnara 9103-G89, 1991).
Yi Chaesuk kayagŭm Sanjo/Lee Chae Suk Kayagum Sanjo: Traditional Folk-art Music (Top JCTOP-008, 1997).
Yi Chaesuk kyosu ch'ŏt yŏnjuro ŭi ch'odae/Collection of Premieres Played by Lee Chae-Suk (Seoul Records SRCD-9644, 2001).

Other Recordings

Listed by date of publication. Romanizations/English translations are given as printed; some CDs lack catalogue numbers.

Hwang Pyŏnggi, *Hwang Pyŏnggi kayagŭm ch'angjak kokchip/Kayagum Pieces by Byung-ki Hwang* (3 LPs: Sung Eum RS069, 1978, RS104, 1979, RS143, 1984) (3 cassettes: CS-072, 1985) (4 CDs: DS034, 1993, DS035, 1993, DS036, 1993, DS037, 1993, and CNLR0103-2 – CNLR0106-2, 2001).
Kim Hae-Sook, *Kugak: Kayagŭm sanjo/Korean Traditional Music Vol. V* (SKC SKCC-K-0010, 1987).
Ppuri kip'ŭn namu sanjo chŏnjip/The Deep-Rooted Tree Sanjo Collection (7 LPs) (The Deep-Rooted Tree Publishing House SELRO 137, 1989).
Yi Sŏngch'ŏn, *Pada* (2 LPs) (Syn-Nara SELRO 187, 1991).
Saeul Kayagŭm Trio, *Sŏul Saeul kayagŭm samjungjudan/Saeul Kayagŭm Trio, Seoul* (SKC SKCD-K-0436, 1992).
Yi Haeshik, *Paramgwa yŏja* (Seoul Records SRB-019, 1992).
Kayagŭm sanjo myŏngindŭl/The Legendary Artists of Korean Kayagŭm Sanjo (5 CDs) (King Records SYNCD-059B – SYNCD-063B, 1993).
Korea: Shamanistic Ceremonies of Chindo (JVC World Sounds (Tokyo) VICG-5214-2, 1993).
Moon Chae-suk [Mun Chaesuk], *Mun Chaesuk kayagŭm sanjo/Kayagŭm Sanjo by Moon, Chae-suk* (SEM DS-0043, 1993).
Yi Sŏngch'ŏn, *Yi Sŏngchŏn kayagŭm chakp'um 1: Pada* (KBS SRCD-1277, 1995).
Chŏng Namhŭi, Kayagŭm sanjo ŭi myŏngindŭl 1: Myŏngch'ang Chŏng Namhŭi, Kayagŭm sanjo, Pyŏngch'ang/Kayagum Sanjo, Byung Chang Performed by Nam Hee Chung (Cantabile SRCD1352, 1996).
Yi Sŏngch'ŏn, *Yi Sŏngchŏn kayagŭm chakp'um 2: Supsok ŭi iyagi/Tales from the Woods* (Seoul Records SRCD-1358, 1996).
Yi Sŏngch'ŏn, *21-hyŏn kayagŭmŭl wihan tokchugok/The Selection of 21 String Kayageum Solo* (Seoul Records SRCD-1359, 1996).

Yang Seung-hee, *Yang Sŭnghŭi kayagŭm sanjo/Yang, Seung-hee Gayagum Sanjo, Juk-pa Version* (Seoul Records SRCD-1399, 1997).

Chŏng Nam-hŭi and Hwang Byungki Sanjo School (*Tchalbŭn kayagŭm sanjo moŭm, Chŏng Namhŭi-je Hwang Pyŏnggi ryu*) (Sung Eum DE-0234, 1998).

Kim Tongjun, *Chŏkpyŏkka* (2 CDs) (Synnara Music NSSRCD-027 and NSSRCD-028, 2000).

Kim Il-ryun, *Kim Illyun ŭi noraehanŭn kayagŭm/Singing Gayageum of Kim Il-ryun* (Seoul Records SRCD-1451, 2001).

Moon Jae Suk, *P'ungnyu* (2 CDs) (Ene Media SCO-170MCS, 2001).

Park Hyun-suk, *Kim Chukp'a ryu, Park Hyŏnsuk Kayagŭm sanjo/Kajagŭm Sanjo* (Synnara Music NSSRCD-036, 2001).

Sagye, *Sagye, kayagŭm ensemble* (Polymedia, 2001).

Yang Seung-Hee, *Kim Ch'angjo sanjo wŏnhyŏng – Yang Sŭnghŭi kayagŭm sanjo/ The History of Yang Seung-Hee – the original kayageum sanjo created by Kim Changjo* (Woongjin, 2001).

Kim Nam Soon, *Kim Namsun kayago/Kim Nam Soon's Kayagŭm* (Seoul Records SRCD-1484, 2002).

Kim Soochul, *Guitar Sanjo* (Living Sound, 2002).

Sookmyung Gayageum Orchestra, *Let it be* (Seoul Records SRCD-1524, 2003).

Sagye, *Kayagŭm angsangbŭl Sagye 2 chip/Kayagum ensemble SAGYE part 2* (Tae Kwang Record/EMI Korea, 2004).

Gayami, *Gaya Beauty Gayageum Trio Vol. 1* (ISMM Records, 2004).

Yi Ji-young, *P'alkae ŭi chŏnggyŏng/8 Scenes: Contemporary Music for Gayageum* (EMI CNLR 0407-2, 2004).

Moon Jae Sook, *Kim Juk P'a Style Kayagŭm Sanjo by Moon Jae Suk* (Seoul Records SRCD-1612, 2005).

Yeoul, *Happy Story/Haengbokhan iyagi* (C&L Music, EMI CNLR0624-2, 2005).

Sookmyung Gayageum Orchestra, *For You* (Seoul Records SRCD-1624, 2006).

Sookmyung Gayageum Orchestra, *Lovely Gayageum* (Seoul Records SRCD-1627, 2006).

Lee Rang, *Family Ensemble 'Lee Rang' 1st Album* (Synnara NSC-172, 2006).

IS (Infinity of Sound), *Step One* (Seoul Records SRCD-3959, 2007).

Index